ENC

"I love *When Lambs Become Lions* because it clearly lays out the potential for every "lamb" to become a "lion." By mixing together the testimonies from many nations while promoting hunger for the Holy Spirit, Dwight has combined for us the explosive ingredients that make the transformation to "lions" possible. Read this book expecting mane to begin growing from your wool. Then be stirred to roar into the nations."

Johnny Enlow
Author of *7 Mountain Prophecy* and *7 Mountain Mantle*

"Dwight Haymon's book, *When Lambs Become Lions*, carries the weight of a life that has witnessed that exact principle. I can't commend this book enough to you. Dwight crafts with words the demonstration of the Father's Love and Heart for His Destiny in your life. I long for books like this that give words to things that generally are difficult to put into words! I was moved through many emotions in this incredible work that, frankly, took me by surprise. I had no idea my friend was such a great writer. I've known Dwight for a little while. I actually met him many years ago as a Vineyard Pastor, but lost touch with him. Recently, the Lord has enabled me to be with Dwight and his wife, Candy, in their home on many occasions. They live what Dwight writes. Though brilliant in scholarly understand- ing and discipline, it is the simplicity and childlike nature of his life that reflects Jesus. The outworking of what he writes in this book carries great value and integrity because he lives it. I was so touched by his honesty, his fears, and his ability to grasp the Father's Love in the midst of so many things that would drive others to run. Dwight carries us along as he runs to Papa God in all the Fullness that God has! He runs regardless of cost...regardless of fear...straight into the arms of The Father. He demonstrates wonderfully how lambs can become lions...how the meek will inherit the earth...because they are the bold ones...the fierce ones...the ones that know they are loved, supported, and encouraged by their Papa, God!"

Danny Steyne
Mountain Of Worship
Author, *When Bruised Reeds Break* and *These Walk on Water*

WHEN LAMBS BECOME LIONS

DWIGHT HAYMON

DEDICATION

While I wrote about the release of the Elijah Generation, two of my grandchildren, *Elias and Ella*, were born. Interestingly enough, their names are derivatives of "Elijah." God confirmed the writing of this book by their names.

I dedicate this book to my two grandchildren, and the ones yet to come. It is my prayer that they will know Papa God and His great love for them.

CONTENTS

ACKNOWLEDGMENTS

I thank Holy Spirit for guiding me in the writing of this book. I learned to hear God in extraordinary ways through the writing process. There were many tears released during the book's creation as Papa overwhelmed me with His Presence. He is good.

As I told the stories throughout this book, I had a number of twenty-somethings in mind. I do appreciate the hundreds who allowed my wife, Candy, and I to be a part of their lives.

My rich heritage of the Word cannot go unmentioned. I am a third generation leader of Christ's church. I have been a pastor for many years and my father, Charles, was an elder and teacher; my grandfather, John, was a deacon. I am so thankful for a dedicated group of people who love the Word. God bless them!

The people closest to me have been so understanding and have given tremendously to the completion of this book. Thank you, Lifegate, for your continuing grace and support of this project. Aimee, thank you for helping in the final, final, final...edit. My children, Jonathan and Barin, Bethany and Buck, and Sarah are a witness and testimony to what God has done. I praise Him for providing this experience of *knowing Him* together.

To Candy: my cheerleader, my editor, the champion of my heart, the witness to the validity of my life, the apple of my eye, my wife: Love!

MALACHI 4:5-6

See, I will send the prophet Elijah to you before that great and dreadful [awesome] day of the Lord comes. He will turn the hearts of the fathers to their children, and the hearts of the children to their fathers; or else I will come and strike the land with a curse.

INTRODUCTION

UNTIL LAMBS BECOME LIONS

"Rise and rise again until lambs become lions."
— Robin Hood, the Movie, 2010

Imprinted on Robin Hood's newfound sword, the words haunted him to the core of his being. When Little John and Will Scarlet asked him what it meant, Robin Hood explained, "It means never give up." Rise, and rise again, until the docile lambs become conquering lions.

The daunting process of gentle lambs becoming mighty lions was a persistent challenge in my life as well. I originally "signed up" because of the love God had shown me nearly forty years ago. Then I found the "more" of Jesus some eighteen years ago. I just wanted to experience His love! I found that His love changes everything! Being a lion is awesome, but you can be a lion with the love of the Father. I had seen "lions" in the Kingdom of God and they seemed ferocious. I wasn't so sure I wanted to eat the little lambs. Then I met Jesus again and again.

Being a lamb isn't wrong! Being one of His lambs is mandatory, but after character is built, it's then time to grow into a formidable opponent in the hand of the Lord. Leif Hetland teaches that the lamb represents alignment and the lion, assignment. We align ourselves in a gentle and humble way with Jesus, then come to realize our purpose with Jesus—to undo the works of the devil "…who prowls around like a roaring lion looking for someone to devour" (1 Pet. 5:8). We become greater lions—lions joined with The Lion of the Tribe of Judah!

Jesus is the great paradox. John saw this in a vision, "Then I saw a Lamb, looking as if it had been slain, standing in the center of the throne..." (Rev. 5:6). Get this: a lamb slain, yet standing. How can this be? Obviously, Jesus died and now the resurrection has brought Him life. Now, He is "...the Lion...who has triumphed" (vs. 5). Jesus showed me this simple gospel message wasn't to be hoarded, but was to be given away.

Papa is doing something! He's changing, awakening, shaking, and shifting the very fiber of our souls for our transformation from little lambs to mighty lions. The day of comfortable Christianity, arranged by man, is over. Papa wants to show you His comfort, His future, His love, His peace, joy, and more! He has destiny written all over you and it is better than anything you can imagine! His love is more than we can think or ask!

Lions know who they are and what they're to do!

To be a lion, joined with the Lion from the Tribe of Judah, is to know your destiny and your future. It is hope realized! It is like a tapestry being knitted together with seemingly flimsy threads, yet its beauty is in the strength and form of the threads woven together. We come to realize the basic truth that God is holding all things together with the super glue of His Power!

Being a Christian is amazing!

Being a Disciple is living a life of direction and purpose!

Being a Son or Daughter is Life! It is an epic journey!

I thank God for my three children. They have watched my wife and me grow and process through life's twists and turns. They are our heritage from the Lord and have always filled our home with life! The Lord has also allowed us to give birth to many spiritual children as well. We like to hang out with the twenty-somethings and they usually seek us out. It's exciting to see God duplicate our insatiable passion for Him in others.

You can be twenty-something or fifty-something. The process of lambs becoming lions is demonstrated in God's release of this *Elijah Generation*. The Elijah Generation is NOW! Its age group is all inclusive. In this prophetic hour, God is bringing us to know Him and His love in order to prepare the way, much like John the Baptizer: "And he will go on before the Lord, in the spirit and power of Elijah, to turn the hearts of the fathers to their children and the disobedient to the wisdom of the righteous—to make ready a people prepared for the Lord" (Luke 1:17). Echoing the last few verses of the Old Testament, these verses set the stage for our destiny before the Lord's return.

Jesus is coming! He is using His end-time army, prepared to move in the power of the Gospel with miracles, signs and wonders, healing the sick, raising the dead, preaching the Gospel, setting the captives free, and…He's calling you! As you read this book, you will feel the Presence of His Holy Spirit. Just say, "Yes!"

My wife, Candy, and I are committed to join with Jesus and help His lambs go to the next step. It would be pretentious of us to think we have all the answers. Let me set that straight. We don't! It is the intent of this book to share stories of how God has changed us and is awakening the people around us. So, let me file the obligatory disclaimer: It is not about me! It is about Jesus! If I ever sound like I'm boasting, I boast in Jesus alone! Candy and I are just ordinary people doing extraordinary things. I invite you to do "the stuff" of Jesus. I invite you to sign up for a lionhearted odyssey!

WHEN LAMBS BECOME LIONS

1

THE ELIJAH GENERATION

The Transformation Begins

"About 40% of our students—if they are pastors—lose their job at their local church after going through this course." These were the words of the highly esteemed and well-known professor of my doctoral class in Church Growth. I really didn't have a clue as to the possible impact of that statement. He continued on, "They may not intentionally get fired, but within six to eight months, there is usually some kind of shakeup—they either change churches or the church changes them." I still wasn't sure about his comments, but I was intrigued. The class was transformational for me and began to fulfill all I had been looking for. You see, God began healing people in this class. After years of theological studies, I was finally in a class that gave me hope to see the real power of God. I had heard about it, but never had I seen it!

"Dwight, you're going to lose your job," my wife exclaimed! I quickly corrected her because I had pastored churches for over twenty years. I know how to work with people and the church I served felt very secure; we had grown from 30 to 300 in about three years. The people were with me and ready for a new phase in our building program. The new multi-purpose building was being planned. We had a dynamic youth program. "I'm not going to get fired," I quipped. I can't get fired; they need me! I couldn't believe her skepticism! Why wouldn't anyone embrace the fact that my foot had just been healed from a year long basketball injury or that I personally watched a leg grow two inches! I mean, really, we had been waiting for this!

I've been waiting on this all my life. I was born for this. I knew there had to be more power somewhere. There had to be more than just praying for a list of people in the Sunday bulletin and really expecting nothing. We would pray for the doctors and the nurses. Why not pray, God, will you heal them? There was such a huge disconnect between the power I preached about and found in the Bible and that which was effectively happening (or not happening) in my ministry. The great chasm between Ephesians 1, Philippians 3, and all of the Gospels, and what I saw in the typical church brought more and more dread in my life. There was a real categorization and separation between the doctrine of God and my relationship with Him. To only know about Him, but *not know Him,* created more confusion, chaos, fear, anger and coldness.

I pray also, that the eyes of your heart may be enlightened in order that you may know…His incomparably great power for us…that power is like the working of His mighty strength, which He exerted in Christ when He raised Him from the dead. (Eph. 1:18-21)

"I want to know Christ and the power of His resurrection…" (Phil. 3:10).

You see, when the Father of this creation shows up in

power, there is relationship and love. My extreme hunger to see God come in power was answered with the power of His love. His love totally surprised me! During this time period, I was asking existential questions about Jesus. I had heart wrenching questions about "love." I understood it conceptually, but I had no clue to its transformational power. Some want to separate Papa's love from His power. I don't see it. I believe that's why 1 Corinthians 13 and 14 go so well together.

WHEN THE FATHER OF CREATION SHOWS UP IN POWER, THERE IS RELATIONSHIP AND LOVE.

I thought I was very successful. I was on a couple of boards in my denomination. I could tell you of the building programs, youth programs, the number of people who had come to Christ and how many perfect attendance pens I had received. I performed really well. I was a good little pastor…but my soul was crying out for more.

Devotions, reading the Bible, praying, worship, and crying out for more will mess you up. PLEASE DON'T DO IT IF YOU DON'T MEAN IT! God will mess you up and out of your chaos, you will find hope, peace, and love. You will learn to hear Him (John 10). You will find identity and destiny. Bill Hybels' book, *Honest to God*, had encouraged me to try journaling and prayer on a regular basis. It worked.

In my search for more of God, I began taking a few classes in local seminaries to begin my doctorate. I finally decided to intentionally embrace a doctorate of ministry in Church Growth at Fuller Theological Seminary. My first class was with Peter Wagner.

The Encounter

Three thousand pages of reading from a select bibliography were necessary for the class, complete with written critiques, followed by written papers after attending a two week seminar. We even had field work to do on the weekends which led me to believe this a bona fide beginning class for this doctoral endeavor. I was a little intimidated, but felt well at ease with the subject of church growth. I was ready to jump in with all I had. In fact, I had previously flown to Orlando months before this February 1994 class to embark upon a seminar on church growth with Dr. Wagner. He made me feel very comfortable with this adventure. I perceived this to be part of my destiny. It just felt right.

The class was great. About thirty-five doctoral achievers were grouped together. Many were pastors, so there was a pragmatic feel in the classroom. Of course, Wagner was a practitioner himself, having been a missionary in Columbia, South America, for years. Moreover, the intellectual exercise was appealing. Wagner had written about fifty books at the time, so he was no academic slouch. Fuller Seminary was, and still is, a world renowned school for movers and shakers. I could tell this was a perfect fit and balance.

Suddenly, I felt like I was on the cutting edge of church growth and missions. We even saw a film of Donald McGavern, a proven missiologist of my past as I had read many of his books in undergraduate school. We were methodically going through a notebook Wagner had prepared, when in the middle of the course, there was something that caught my attention. My eyes fell on the middle tab of the notebook, "Spiritual Gifts Can Help Your Church Grow." That was our next module for the afternoon!

We went through the lesson, well prepared and backed by Scripture. I agreed with most everything Dr. Wagner taught and it really brought life to what I believed, fleshing out some unorganized thoughts that I had for years. Being a "tongue-tied charismatic" at that season of my life, I found myself agreeing with Dr. Wagner as he taught. Of course, I believed in healing. Of course, I believed in prophecy. This lesson just affirmed what I believed, or so I thought.

However, I wasn't prepared for what happened next. As Dr. Wagner taught, he began to tell stories. Oh, the stories! If he'd only kept everything in theory, everything would have been ok. If we can keep the power and the anointing confined to a time that has now past, then everything would be fine. No, he was about to release something that would change my life forever. Let me say that again: FOREVER!

God is very controllable when left in the printed Word, but when He is made flesh, it really becomes a problem for all of us who like observing from a distance. The incarnation of God through Jesus Christ, His Son, created enough of a storm in the religious community 2000 years ago. Let's not let Him do that again! But wait, He wants to do it again through His Holy Spirit—making Jesus real and alive today! Opening Pandora's box is a pedantic and anemic cliché compared to what was about to occur. The testimony of Jesus was about to set the captives free! This was what I was created for.

Dr. Wagner began telling stories about his God-given spiritual gift of healing. Not a general gift of healing, but a specific gift of healing. His specialty, it seemed, was backs and legs. God healed through Wagner, especially in the problem areas of backs and legs! After hearing several testimonies, I was a believer. I mean, he couldn't make this stuff up! There were just too many nuances and situations that would be hard to cover. He shared with us about his Sunday School class of over 100 and how many had been healed in it, and also a class he taught on "Signs and Wonders" with John Wimber, father of the Vineyard. Once Wagner was at a banquet and the Lord told him to heal them all, so he did. All got healed in one setting. Over 50 people received God's healing power out of a room of about 300. Really?!!

Wagner was no TV evangelist. He was professorial, intelligent. He didn't fit the mold of a "faith healer" stereotype. And yet, this—an incredible, relational expression of God with healing power. At the end of class one day, I remember him saying, "By the way, if anyone has a problem with backs and legs, we'll heal them in the morning during devotions and prayer." He stated it simply, naturally and unpretentiously.

I had been set up. Holy Spirit had heard my cries and declarations from the pulpit that *there had to be more*. One year earlier, I had sprained my ankle while playing basketball. My ankle ligaments were torn. To this day, I remember hearing my ligaments tear as if they were connected to my head. It was that severe. Over the course of the year, I had been to several doctors, relied on crutches, and then a cane, cried out of frustration, and finally, accepted my lot in life to walk with a limp. Though I was mostly healed, my foot had been relegated to some atrophy. I couldn't bend my toes. My foot was numb most of the time with the exception of a tingling sensation due to a lack of blood flow.

The next morning, the blood flowed—the Blood of Jesus! At eight o'clock, just like usual, we began class with a short reading of Scripture and prayer led by one of the seminarians. Again, Wagner pointed out that we would pray for anyone with back and leg problems and if that didn't work, he would go one-on-one during the morning break. All of us prayed, led by one of the students. The power of God fell in the room. I felt the power of God go from the top of my head to the end of my right foot and for the first time in a year, I could bend my toes. Praise God! To this day, I still get emotional telling the story, overwhelmed by His love! That was enough to change me, but I was, unknowingly, set on a crash course with the Holy Spirit! Originally, I thought the purpose of the class was a means to get another degree on the wall, or build a bigger church. However, the Kingdom of God was at hand!

One guy didn't get healed. Well, of course not; he walked with a limp and had an inch and a half build up on his shoe. He was a nice guy, a pastor in the Salvation Army, with some ranking denoted by the decorations on his uniform. As with the rest of the class, we all came from a cornucopia of places. A buddy to my right was an American Baptist from California and a buddy to my left was a Lutheran from up north. The decorated Salvation Army social gospel officer/pastor was from Pittsburgh. Since his foot wasn't healed, Wagner reiterated, "We'll go one-on-one with you during the break." "This I gotta see," I thought.

And see, I did! When class let out for our fifteen-minute break, the officer made his way to the front. Many were milling about; some were even walking down the hallway. Not me! I could not miss this. Wagner asked Phil to sit down. As he sat down, I moved closer. I wanted front row seating. I was stooped over him, jockeying for sideline positioning. I was about three feet away from him, just enough to give him a comfortable social forbearance of space, but not enough to allow anyone else to pull in front of me. I was there! I had to see this!

Wagner bent down and the words I heard still echo in my mind to this day, "I praise you Heavenly Father for all that you are doing in this place and now I command this leg to grow in the name of Jesus Christ." It was a simple prayer with incomparable power to follow. The leg grew! I saw it! I saw it grow instantaneously before my very eyes. Never before had I seen anything happen like that. Wagner didn't shout. He spoke naturally with supernatural power and authority. It was effortlessly done in about two minutes! …Pause… Let it soak in. I wish you could have been there! The eternal ramifications of this moment were going to shake the foundations of hell and shake loose the power of God!

I told my wife. She unknowingly prophesied, "You're going to lose your job." "But honey, I cannot deny what has happened to me; I'm a changed man." She knew it by my voice. More had happened in that room than the healing of my foot or Phil's leg growing before my very eyes. Jesus was in the room. The power of God was so strong my heart was being changed. When pure glory and love show up in the room, it transforms your spirit, body, and soul. The Light had shown up. I was changed forever. No longer was I to argue why "God doesn't do those kinds of things today." The veil had been torn. The Father's Heart was released.

Phil, too, was in a conundrum. His denomination didn't totally embrace supernatural healing either. He had several of us who witnessed the miracle write letters to his captain, confirming what happened. He had to go buy a new pair of shoes; the specially made, built-up shoe no longer worked for him. He was healed miraculously!

God did quite a lot during those two weeks of class. For instance, I was no longer a tongue-tied charismatic. After joining a small group of pastors from various places and various faiths or denominations, once again, I found Light of Revelation. For years I had argued against speaking in tongues. This argument was about to come to an end. As we prayed, one person spoke in tongues and the apparent leader of the group asked, "Who has the interpretation? Who has it? Dwight, do you have it?" Well, I'd never heard God like that, but I described what I saw and heard. They exclaimed, "That's it! You have the interpretation!" From that moment, I realized why there are tongues. It is just another form of revelation. It made perfect sense. For the first time, tongues made sense even though it usually sounds so chaotic. God brings order out of chaos!

What I discovered during that class was much more than I bargained for. After leaving the class, I preached the Kingdom of God. I told stories of God's supernatural and miraculous power and people responded in a great way. Over thirty people responded to the message that next Sunday morning at the church I served. People's lives were being changed, and so was mine. Later, incredible healings began to occur. God was doing so much and I wanted more. He seems to always give us enough to stir a desire for more and I wanted more!

The Exit

Let me first praise God for a tremendous Bible-based background I received through my denominational heritage. Often, there is a weak foundation for many "experience-led religions." I'm so blessed to have the Word in my life! My denomination, while limiting the power of the Holy Spirit, helped me grow and mature. I was given a strong foundation in the Word. I appreciate my rich heritage of the Bible.

Grappling with issues of doctrine and trying to process

all that was new to me, I needed help. Jack Deere's book, *Surprised by the Power of the Holy Spirit*, is a great help in methodically answering many questions that a faithful student of the Word may have. Remember my background! I needed Biblical understanding for these new experiences. Deere's book became a compendium for me when others challenged my faith and departure from the denomination. Even Deere had to leave his denomination and his teaching position at Dallas Seminary.[1] I was so hungry for a new framework in order to understand and process all that God was doing. I read this book in about six hours on a Friday night. I couldn't put it down. The Lord had placed this book in my hand at just the right time. It was a much needed understanding for what was to come.

More changes were in the works. The tradition I was a part of just couldn't allow the powerful healings that took place week after week. There was no theological grid within my denomination for what I had become, nor for the evident signs of God's power. The "shoe just doesn't fit anymore," as one elder put it. I forgave the elders, as well as my pastor friend who implored me to repent from this charismatic stuff. I forgave a leader of leaders who, while in a pastors' meeting, stated, "We lost another one to the charismatic movement" (speaking of me). I didn't know I was lost. In fact, I felt like I was found! I had gained so much! I was moving on from glory to glory. I had moved into realms that made even the charismatic community doubtful. I wasn't charismatic, nor was I Pentecostal. God was doing a new thing. I later learned that God was moving in a "third wave" of the Holy Spirit and I was a part of that. I didn't feel like I was a part of the "Holy Ghost" traditions of the past. God was doing something new through other groups, outpourings in Toronto, Brownsville,

Kansas City IHOP, and other places around the world. God says, "See, I am doing a new thing!" (Isa. 43:19); I wanted to be a part of it!

After completing my course with Dr. Wagner, I studied under him again in June of 1994. This was a powerful session on prayer. Through prayer, God was about to move me into a new arena, free to flow in the Holy Spirit. Prayer had become a key to my life. I was praying about two to three hours a day. I met weekly with a few pastors and we really prayed. Notice, it wasn't one of those "prayer breakfasts" where you do everything but pray. I also met weekly for prayer with three intercessors. I've often told them that they prayed me right out of my job! And so it was. The exit was about to take place.

Bizarre things began to occur. The elders asked me to stop talking about healing. No one ever knew that God told me, "If you stop talking about healing, then I will stop doing it." I had been given a greater mandate. Next, an impromptu Thursday morning meeting was scheduled with the whole church. Strange accusations were thrown toward me. I was accused of becoming proud, trying to take all the credit for what was happening. One comment was, "He just doesn't listen anymore!" (Loosely, translated, "I can't control him anymore.") I could go on and on. Day after day, the accusations continued and, eventually, wore me down. The pinnacle of this nonsense came when a church member wrote a nine-page paper on "Why the Church does not use oil anymore." That one blew me away. Again, it was becoming quite bizarre. I knew the father of lies was behind this debacle. I really only write this to show the ludicrous ploys the enemy uses to accuse and divide. My intent is not to judge or portray any kind of bitterness. I have forgiven, many times, all who were involved in the mess. You need to know when bad things happen to good people, it's only a test! Great things are about to happen even in the midst of the chaos.

As the heat really began to fire up during this whole situation, I recalled my wife's declaration, "You're going to get fired!" On this side of the situation, it was the best thing in the world that ever happened to me. However, during the heat of the moment, I was broken. God was about to convey His love and faithfulness in ways I had never known. As the church was preparing to sever relationship, Papa was about to bring on true relationship! The verdict was rendered, and I had to leave. The church gave me a "severance package." I was given two months severance pay following my resignation.

During the severance period, someone told me that the word "severance" is associated with the grisly history of the guillotine. As you know, the guillotine was a bloody tool that severed the head from the body. *Sever* is defined as breaking off or separating by cutting. I saw a parallel with John the Baptizer's beheading (Matt. 14:1-12). John was the Forerunner, the Elijah spirit mentioned in Malachi 4:5. His head was severed in an attempt to stop the power and impact of his message. Many forerunners have gone through trial, punishment, and suffering, even to the point of death, because of the message they brought. Paul, John, and many others who brought an anti-religious message about Christ, had to suffer. The norm, however, is to bring an anti-Christ message about religion. God is calling forth the Elijahs, the John the Baptizers, the forerunners on this glorious day. This is the season to rise up, count the cost, take up your cross, deny yourself, and follow Him.

Pure gold is produced spectacularly through the fire.

Candy and I have seen thousands of healings and tens of thousands of prophetic words given. We have been a part of many new church plantings worldwide. We train leaders how to hear God and to do Kingdom "stuff" internationally. We work with many twenty-something year olds, projecting them into the Kingdom. We've seen the lame walk, the blind see, and the prisoner set free. We've seen many demons flee, many baptized, many receive Christ, many baptized in the Holy Spirit, many inner healings. I would never have experienced this if I had not been set free from the fear of man and religion. The left foot of Christian fellowship actually kick-started me into a whole new realm!

This is what Jesus did. This is what Elijah did—and John the Baptizer, the Forerunner. And now you! You are destined to do the things that Jesus did and more: "I tell you the truth, anyone who has faith in me will do what I have been doing. He will do even greater things than these..." (John 14:12).

The Entreaty

The entreaty placed upon my life was to know the Father and His heart for any situation.

> See, I will send you the prophet Elijah before that great and dreadful day of the Lord comes. He will turn the hearts of the fathers to their children, and the hearts of the children to their fathers or else I will come and strike the land with a curse.
> (Mal. 4:5-6)

With very little understanding of the meaning of this scripture, I continually received this message from recognized people who hear from God. Whether large arenas or small, people consistently gave me this message, "You have the Father's Heart." I began to study and entreat the Lord concerning these words. More and more revelation came forth as I studied and cried out to Him. It became apparent that I had a message to give. So, this entreaty became encouragement to others as I shared the Father's Heart.

Peru became a training ground for me during the beginning of the new century. The message of the Father's Heart became more prevalent. I had it to give away. People were changed by the glory of God when I preached about Papa's love. I found myself preaching in Lima to a fairly large crowd one Father's Day with the message of the Father's Heart. I remembered a great revival breaking out in Brownsville, Florida, on Father's Day just a few years prior. I wondered…would you do it again, Lord?

As I began preaching, I could tell I had a good translator! That is so crucial. I got in a flow, starting the next sentence before the translator finished the last sentence. The downtime was kept to a minimum between my words and the translation. There was plenty of time to think before I formed the next sentence, making it succinct and clear the first time. We had it going! It was like paddling a canoe—every time you stroke with your paddle, you do it with the same congruence as your partner who is also paddling, thus gently getting the boat down the river. This was what was happening with my translator; it was smooth.

However, something huge had happened! Halfway into my sermon, I realized that she had read something different than my passage of Malachi 4:5-6. Somehow, she heard Malachi 3:5-6, which speaks of judgment against sorcerers, adulterers, perjurers, and those who oppress their workers, widows, and people that can't help themselves. Here I was preaching on the Father's Heart of love and the sermon had been preceded by a call to repentance. When I noticed the replacement of Scriptures, I corrected the reference, and then began to see the correlation between the two citings.

While the two appeared to be in opposition to one another, actually the correlation of the two seemed to be a central theme of Elijah coming forth in the New Testament via John the Baptizer and Jesus. When you put the two together, you could have the following entreaty of the Gospels: Repent, for the Kingdom is at hand! In essence, I had inadvertently said, "If you want His love, you have to repent!" Many times, revelation comes when you least expect it and in the most unusual places. I was in Peru, declaring this Word, when we were suddenly diverted to a greater revelation of the Father's Kingdom!

I asked my interpreter to please read the Malachi 4 passage. As she read the Scripture, revelation and power came. People began wailing and crying! I heard "no small stir" (Acts 12:18) in the crowd. I preached with my whole heart and then the ministry team began to pray for people to receive Papa's heart. We had prophetic words for people and Holy Spirit was ministering powerfully. At one point, I imparted Papa's love over the whole crowd. I noticed my interpreter stopped translating. She had done a good job and I thought she was tired or, perhaps, getting a drink of water. I looked around to see what she was doing.

My interpreter was gone! She had "fallen out." In other words, she was overcome with God's presence and had collapsed onto the stage. Now what do I do? I have no interpreter. From that moment on, although there were no words spoken that could be understood mentally, I felt assured that everyone in the room had understanding in the Spirit (see 1 Cor. 14:15). God did so much through His language and His presence. It's amazing when you don't need an interpreter because Holy Spirit is the interpreter! People experienced a real revival that day. Praise God!

One of the takeaways from that day was a revelation about the Kingdom of God. Yes, it was new and it was old. Throughout the Old Testament you see the judgments of God, but if you continue to read, His mercy does triumph over judgment. Papa's heart was, and is, always entreating us to repentance and restoration. If His people will repent, then He will heal their land (2 Chron. 7:14). Today, He wants to bless the land—US! God is good and His desire for us is to be blessed, free from sin, free from shackles of every kind.

> The Spirit of the Sovereign Lord is on me...He has sent me to bind up the brokenhearted, to proclaim freedom for the captives and release from darkness for the prisoners, to proclaim the year of the Lord's favor...to comfort all who mourn... (Isa. 61:1-3)

How trite? No, not really. Jesus died on the cross. Why? He loves us and He wants us to be free. As we become free, we free others. We are competent ministers, equipped for every good work. He is raising a passionate generation that is ready to go anywhere and do anything for Papa. There is an Elijah Generation coming forth to be the Forerunners of Jesus' coming again. They will preach the good news of the Kingdom. They will hear Papa's voice and be able to do whatever is needed for any occasion. This generation, youth and aged alike, is unstoppable! "From the days of John the Baptist until now, the Kingdom of heaven has been forcefully advancing, and forceful men lay hold of it" (Matt. 11:12).

I pray this book will open pathways that haven't been open before. I pray that as you read this book, every mountain will be put asunder and every valley will be filled (Isa. 40:4). I pray that the eyes of your heart will be opened to see God and His great power! I pray you will see that you are a part of this Elijah Generation. You are becoming a lion!

THE TRANSFORMATION FROM LAMBS TO LIONS IS REALLY ABOUT THE FATHER'S HEART.

Perhaps through the inspiration, the exhortation, the stories, the instruction, and the impartation, God will move you closer into the realms of glory! You are really called for this. As you read this, I pray you will realize that God is calling you. I pray that His supplication, the Holy Spirit's entreaty for you, is realized and you get up, repent and say: "Lord Jesus, I commit my life to you; use me and make me to be a blessing everyday. I want to be called for your special purpose. The passion I have received from you is to bring your Kingdom to earth. Make me ready to help make you ready. Use this epiphany, this revelation that you are giving me to help bring about the greatest eschatological event of all times: 'LORD JESUS, COME!' "

Hey, Jesus is coming back soon! The Elijah Generation is coming forth to preach the good news about His Kingdom. It's all about forgiveness and His love! Now, let's go do it. The transformation from lambs to lions is really about the Father's Heart.

---

1. Jack Deere, *Surprised By the Power of the Spirit.* (Grand Rapids: Zondervan, 1993), p. 37.

2
I WANT THAT!

There's a "Tupperware scene" in the movie, *Napoleon Dynamite*. If you remember, Napoleon's uncle is giving his sales pitch to a married couple in the neighborhood. As he impressively wrapped up his presentation, the wife's response was one of euphoric declaration, "I want that." You have to see the movie, but that's what I decided in my doctoral class of 1994. I knew this is what I wanted and I went after it. Sure, it was a serious thing, but with God leading the way, it was fun!

Maybe to you, being a forerunner means that you eat locusts and wild honey, but for me, it has been a blast. I have had a lot of fun with Papa; the more I got to know Him, the more fun He became. That may blow up your box, but the Creator of heaven and earth is really fun to hang out with. No, no, don't lose me now. If you want to get all serious and tied up, ok, you can do that, but I'm telling you that God shows Himself to you the way He needs to. "To the pure you show yourself pure, but to the devious you show yourself shrewd" (Ps. 18:26). For me, the past seventeen years have been the ride of my life. Yes, it has been very serious at times, but it has also been a lot of fun!

I've been in a variety of places—Peru, Africa, Dominican Republic, Honduras, Jordan, Lebanon, India, Jamaica, Ireland, restaurants, shopping centers, bars, the marketplace, work, everywhere—and the Kingdom of God has come! It has been a fantastic time! Being a forerunner is bringing the Kingdom of God to earth NOW! Learning Papa's heart for every occasion is really a blast. It is a "high" of revelation that will not allow me to come down. I went up to His holy mountain and He came down! I don't want to leave! This is where I stand and you can, too.

While traveling near Saposoa, Peru, near the "high jungle," Johnny Enlow was traveling with a group through some small villages. The group had spread out through the village to some extent while Johnny talked to some of the villagers. I heard Johnny yell at me, "Hey Dwight, you want to cast out a demon?" Of course, I did! We approached a house to meet a man who couldn't speak. He had been to the witch doctor to get help on several occasions. The family told us that the man hadn't spoken for two weeks. We began praying for him. As we prayed, waiting for discernment, we got a word of knowledge that he had a "deaf and dumb spirit." We began rebuking the spirit! Then the man spoke! He said, "I'm not going to speak." We asked why? He said again, "I'm not going to speak!" Johnny said, "That's the dumbest 'deaf and dumb' spirit I've ever met." We laughed and cut up, rebuked it in the name of Jesus and the man began to speak again. He was cured. Praise God! I WANT THAT!

Now that was fun! I want to do that again! And I have…and so can you! Here is the challenge: Just as John the

Baptizer was the forerunner when Jesus graced this earth in bodily form, God is now calling us to be the forerunners for Christ's return. The Elijah Generation will carry the Father's Heart. Instead of just preaching on the street corner, you can release His Kingdom wherever you go.

A few years ago, Candy and I were teaching and training our first class of twenty-somethings. This was a four-month intensive, equipping in the power of the Holy Spirit with a trip to Africa at the end of the course. As part of the internship, we traveled to North Carolina to attend a conference. One night after the meeting, we went to the local IHOP, high caloric pancakes and all. Naturally, we were going to minister to the server. After receiving our food, I broke the cadence of everyone shoveling in massive quantities of bread covered with syrup. "Okay, now ask Holy Spirit for a 'word' for our waitress. Let's just bless her with the Father's Heart." Within five minutes, our server came with more caffeine juice. I started the ball rolling with a prophetic word, and then others joined in. By the time the fourth person had spoken, our server was in tears. By the fifth or sixth, she ran off in tears. After composing herself, she came back and said, "You just don't know, you just don't know. How did you know all I was going through? This gave me so much hope and now I know that He cares." She had been touched by the Father's Heart. She had encountered the Elijah Generation bringing forth the Kingdom of God—love.

Two weeks prior to this, we were at a Waffle House after a meeting in Charlotte. The Holy Spirit told us some things about our server and we shared what Papa was saying. Have you ever seen a grown man cry? He had tears of joy and appreciation, knowing that God had not given up on him. "How did you know that?" he asked. Then he exclaimed,

"You just don't know what I've been going through." He was obviously taken aback by the power released in the room and in his spirit.

THE KINGDOM OF GOD COMES IN POWER WITH THE TOUCH OF PAPA'S HEART.

This goes on all the time! Everywhere we go! The Kingdom of God comes in power with the touch of Papa's heart. EVERYWHERE! ALL THE TIME! We simply said, "I want that!"

In the context of Malachi 4, we find destruction and judgment for the evildoer, but for you who are reading this book, Malachi says that Jesus will shine on you with "healing in His wings." And you will go out "like calves released from the stall." And then,

> See, I will send you the prophet Elijah before that great and dreadful day of the Lord comes. He will turn the hearts of the fathers to their children, and the hearts of the children to their fathers; or else I will come and strike the land with a curse.
> (Mal. 4:5-6)

Therefore, our opportunity is to bless the land with the Father's Heart as He restores the children's hearts back to His own. We have an awesome opportunity to join Jesus in this incredible work!

Malachi 3:1 sets the scene for John the Baptizer with, "See, I will send my messenger who will prepare the way before me." This prophecy is confirmed and realized in Matthew 3:1ff, "John...preached, 'Repent, for the Kingdom of heaven is near.' This is spoken through the prophet Isaiah:

'A voice of one calling in the desert, prepare the way for the Lord, make straight paths for him.' " The prophecy of Malachi and Isaiah (40:3) is realized! John the Baptizer is the forerunner and is now called the Elijah (Matt. 11:11-15). "From the days of John the Baptizer until now, the Kingdom of heaven has been forcefully advancing, and forceful men lay hold of it. Now...he is the Elijah who was to come." Jesus was not the Elijah (Mark 8: 28; John 1:21). Before the time of Jesus, embedded in Jewish tradition even in the Passover meal, was an understanding known by every Jew. That is, Elijah would have to come before the Messiah would appear on the earth. There had to be a forerunner to announce a clear call for Christ's coming.

Now at the transfiguration (Matt. 17:11-13; Mark 9:12-13), three time periods regarding the coming of Elijah are pointed out by Jesus. Please notice "the old Elijah has come" as he shows up at the transfiguration. Jesus also says that "he has already come" (i.e.., John the Baptizer) and He says, "He will come again and restore all things." Granted, the context is referring to John the Baptizer as the Elijah, but could Jesus be referring to the Second Advent? Just as Matthew 24 is a mixture of prophecies of His coming return and the destruction of Jerusalem, could this not be of the same genre? Could it be that Jesus is showing His hand, showing a pearl, alluding to an event that a new Elijah will come forth just before Jesus returns? Could it be that Jesus is about to "double down" with John the Baptist, the forerunner, once again by calling you?

God is not bound by time. During the transfiguration, where did Moses and Elijah come from anyway? They were seen in recognizable bodily form. Could God have gone back about 2000 years and borrowed Moses for a few minutes and then moved forward 500 years to pick up Elijah and then brought them both to the transfiguration? Isn't that possible with God? Yes, even more so because God is God, the Almighty One, and He is not bound by time! Throughout Jesus' life, He announced that the Kingdom of God is near, the Kingdom of heaven is at hand, is coming, and is within you. Then He says to pray for the Kingdom to come in the Lord's prayer. He is not bound by time and neither is this prophecy about the forerunner coming before Christ comes.

In the Old Testament prophecies about Jesus' coming, the people of old often had little understanding of the true meaning of the prophecies. Many of the Old Testament prophecies Paul used in his arguments in the book of Romans had little to do with his polemic. In fact, it appeared that he was totally ripping the words out of context, yet those words stand today. See, there is certain timeliness to prophecy and a timelessness as well. During the milieu in which the prophecy was given, it fit the time period perfectly. Later, in the New Testament, the prophecy is used in a different time period, but because of the unique characteristic of God's Word, it is not bound to the former time period. The words spoken by Jesus, "Elijah will come again," were a timely word for the context of the transfiguration, but, again, not bound by time. "He will come again" is a call for each generation to pray and cry out for His Kingdom to come. It is a call for each generation to rise up and become forerunners working with Jesus to **prepare** the bride. "I saw the Holy City, the new Jerusalem, coming down out of heaven from God, **prepared** as a bride beautifully dressed for her husband" (Rev. 21:2). "For the wedding of the Lamb has come, and his bride has made herself ready (or **prepared**)" (Rev. 19:7).

The **preparation** of the bride is being released. We are

the new Elijah Generation, helping **prepare** the bride for readiness. After Matthew 17 and the transfiguration, Jesus begins His treatise on the Kingdom parables. He calls us to be ready and **prepared** to enter the Kingdom of heaven by becoming like a little child (Matt. 18:3). The shepherd goes after the lost sheep who is not **prepared** (18:12). The heart has to be **prepared** with forgiveness to enter the Kingdom (18:35). The rich young ruler is told to go and sell his possessions (19:16). The son must be obedient (21:28ff). Jesus urges us to compel people to come to the wedding banquet (Ch. 22). The wedding was ready but the invited guests were not **prepared**. The parable of the ten virgins is all about **preparedness** (Ch. 25). The one who squandered his talents was not **prepared** to enter the Kingdom of heaven. Then in Matthew 25:31, it is the sheep who are called and **prepared** and who will enter the Kingdom. After the transfiguration, the Master's message was to **prepare** the way! The Kingdom of God is NOW! The harvest is ready; pray for the workers—the forerunners!

It's interesting to note that before our Savior breathed His last breath, many thought He cried out for Elijah. The Scriptures are clear that he was saying something else, "Eloi, Eloi, lama sabachthani?" meaning, "My God, my God, why have you forsaken me?" (Mark 15:34-36). But why is this particular sentence written in their spoken language, Aramaic? Could it be that Jesus had a second meaning? Often a heavenly language can be spoken and many hear it in a different way (see the Day of Pentecost: Acts 2). Could it be that with a different language, Jesus was calling for the Elijahs to come forth? Perhaps He was calling for those who would heed His call. He knew that there would be some who would unfold this mystery before His Second coming. He who has an ear, let him hear what the Spirit is saying. "The spirit and the bride say, 'Come!' And let him who hears say, 'Come!' (Rev. 22:17). Let the Lion of the tribe of Judah call this Elijah Generation to be the lions before Jesus comes.

I want that! I want to see His Kingdom come now! We did not sign up for a salvation insurance policy to lock in a safe for redemption some time! The Kingdom of God is now for this Elijah Generation, a generation that moves in signs and wonders. We hear God and do what we see Papa doing (John 5:19). We are equipped for every good work—NOW! There will be healings and miracles everywhere we go because He said to pray like this: "Your Kingdom come, your will be done on earth as it is in heaven" (Matt. 6:10). We bring Jesus to the neighborhood, the nation, and the world. He is the answer. We saturate the land with the redemption of Jesus, the Anointed One. Finally, we call out, "Come!" We agree with you, Spirit, "COME!" And, then, a new heaven!

Even the early church fathers were aware of this forerunner spirit. The call for the Elijah Generation was seen just a few years after the time of Christ:

St. Justin Martyr
If therefore Scripture compels you to admit that two advents of Christ were predicted to take place,— one in which He would appear suffering, and dishonoured, and without comeliness; but the other in which He would come glorious and Judge of all, as has been made manifest in many of the fore-cited passages,— shall we not suppose that the word of God has proclaimed that Elijah shall be the precursor of the great and terrible day, that is, of His second advent?[1]

St. Hippolytus

It is a matter of course that His forerunners must appear first, as He says by Malachi and the angel, Or it may be, "Malachi, even the messenger." "I will send to you Elias the Tishbite before the day of the Lord, the great and notable day, comes; and he shall turn the hearts of the fathers to the children, and the disobedient to the wisdom of the just, lest I come and smite the earth utterly." Mal. iv. 5, 6. These, then, shall come and proclaim the manifestation of Christ that is to be from heaven; and they shall also perform signs and wonders, in order that men may be put to shame and turned to repentance for their surpassing wickedness and impiety.[2]

You and I signed on for the more, not the less! We agree with the Spirit and say, yes, bring your glory; prepare me to prepare others! Let me be a part of that Elijah Generation! His forerunners must appear first. Heed the call!

YOU MAY BE A FORERUNNER IF:

- You have tasted the Lord and know He is good!
- You have seen Him in His Sanctuary and know there is more.
- You may feel like you are in a matrix and you know there is more to life than these random cycles.
- You feel like you have more to offer than anyone recognizes, but you are stuck in a box of theology that regulates you to be a mere history teacher of the Bible.
- You know if you don't break out of the neutralization of the church and the sterilization of God, the fire in your belly will explode

- When you worship, you are disparaged by the gross disconnect between the power of the gospel and the impotence you display in your life.
- You long for the release of Kingdom power in every part of your life—on Monday as well as Sunday.
- You have seen God work; you have heard other people's stories and now, you want your own.

Sound like you? Then, get ready, God is calling you to be a forerunner!

God's Holy Spirit is now releasing preparation for the way of the Lord. He is coming, and out of His mercy He is raising up a generation for a Great Awakening! He is equipping this generation to prepare a right response to Jesus during these End Times by making His plans known. God is releasing us to prepare the way of the Lord regardless of our eschatological views. The Jews are still looking for the Messiah. The Muslims are looking for Him—even to the point where one sect actually has a large pocket sewn in their tunics to receive the man-child when he is birthed. Most religions are looking for the Messiah! We, who name Jesus Christ as our Savior, have the Messiah. He has come and is coming again. A clarion call has been given to this generation to prepare the way for the Lord!

There is an intensity to the time in which we live. Cataclysmic events are occurring and 2 Timothy 3:1-9 is being fulfilled. We are living in epic times, whereby, heroes of the faith are urged to heed the call. They are writers, preachers, teachers, evangelists. They are people in the media, in business, in college, and at home. They are artists, politicians, marketplace workers, and so on. These brothers and sisters in Christ know something big is about to happen. They feel it in their bones.

"Mercy ministries" and "ministries of helps" are rising up all over the world. These ministries are bringing the paradoxical love of the Father. As the intensity of the times explodes—unemployment, dysfunction, obsessions, and upheaval of every kind—Believers are reaching out and bringing healing. We bring life to dying situations. We bring mercy instead of judgment. There will be many who emphasize the judgment of God and who sit on the sidelines. Forerunners are called to bring life, light, and love in all situations. We bring freedom to the prisoner and release to the captive (Isa. 61:1).

A forerunner is a partner with Christ. We are co-laborers with Him. We do what we see the Father doing. We are well equipped to heal the sick, cast out the devil, and raise the dead. It's that simple. We are to do the things that Jesus did.

> I tell you the truth, anyone who has faith in me
> will do what I have been doing He will do even
> greater things than these, because I am going to the
> Father. And I will do whatever you ask in my name,
> so that the Son may bring glory to the Father. You
> may ask me for anything in my name, and I will do it.
> (John 14:12-14)

God births things in prayer. Revivals and awakenings begin in a lifestyle of prayer and fasting. God is releasing intercession, not for the sake of intercession alone, but for His glory and purposes! There are prayer movements around the world. Everlasting purposes are always birthed in prayer. Forerunners see the need to be networked in some kind of prayer movement. Movement is the operative word here.

The real emphasis for the forerunner is the love of the Father. We are to bring His love to every situation because we are constantly walking in His Kingdom. Kingdom life is not something we do; it is who we are. We are His sons and daughters living and walking in His Presence, obeying His good will.

KINGDOM LIFE IS NOT SOMETHING WE DO; IT IS WHO WE ARE.

You and I were designed for a slice of this pie! And it is sooooooooo sweet. You thought it would look differently; well, so did I. This Spirit God has put in us has molded us for such a time as this. See, you were in control in the beginning, but now you aren't—"not my will, but Yours." God has purged you from everything that can keep you away from your inheritance. You no longer let circumstances and other people stand in the way. Cultural setbacks, bitterness, and selfishness are all gone. God prepares forerunners in the wilderness. You may have thought you were broken and left for dead, but no, there is resurrection. You are created for this time and our cry agrees with Paul, "I want to know Christ and the power of His resurrection and the fellowship of sharing in His sufferings…" (Phil. 3:10).

Forerunners have their eyes open and they hear the Father's voice. "The sheep know the voice of the Shepherd" (John 10). So, I pray like Paul,

I keep asking that the God of our Lord Jesus Christ, the glorious Father, may give you the Spirit of wisdom and revelation, so that you may know him better. I pray also that the eyes of your heart may be enlightened in order that you may know the hope to which he has called you, the riches of his glorious inheritance in the saints, and his incomparably great power for us who believe. That power is like the

working of his mighty strength, which he exerted in Christ when he raised him from the dead and seated him at his right hand in the heavenly realms, far above all rule and authority, power and dominion, and every title that can be given, not only in the present age but also in the one to come.
(Eph. 1: 17-21)

As a forerunner, you are a force to be reckoned with. You are a formidable lion. You are a wrecking ball against the forces of evil and you bring salvation to the heart of a person by Words of Life! God's power is beautifully manifested in you. I want that!

MORE LORD!

1. Trypho 49 http://www.newadvent.org/fathers/01284.htm Fathers of the Church: Dialogue with Trypho (Justin Martyr).
2. On the Antichrist
http://www.ccel.org/ccel/schaff/anf05.iii.iv.ii.i.html?scrBook=Mal&scrCh=4&scrV=5#iii.iv.ii.i-p152.1 Christian Classics Ethereal Library, www.ccel.org Treatise on Christ and Antichrist #46 footnote 1496.

3

TEN THOUSAND DOLLARS PLUS

One day last year, as my wife and I were teaching a class on how to hear God, it dawned on me that we had spent tens of thousands of dollars on learning how to hear and encounter the supernatural Holy Spirit. After leaving the denominational church and enrolling in the "school of the Spirit," Candy and I went to Toronto several times, Brownsville in Pensacola, Kansas City (Mike Bickle), St. Louis (Randy Clark). We traveled to Charlotte dozens of times to hang out at Morning Star and Mahesh Chavda Ministries, receiving teaching from the likes of John Paul Jackson, Bill Johnson, Jane Hamon, Larry Randolph, and more. Wherever there was a river flowing from the Lord's throne, we ran toward it (see: Ezek. 47:3-12).

Receiving the Father's Heart

"I don't fit this and I don't think I want to." Those were Candy's thoughts as we walked into a room filled with 3000 seekers in Toronto, Canada. Yet, that was the place where Papa's heart came crashing into ours in a beautiful explosion!

It was October 1994. We were at the Catch the Fire Conference and we had no idea what to expect. We had just begun a Vineyard Fellowship only three months after being extricated from the religious world. Suddenly, we knew we were created for this—this move of God. I have to admit that it looked odd. It did not fit in our box, and I must say, we really didn't want it to. We had been on a bus for about twenty hours with a bunch of people we barely knew who were hungry for the Lord. They seemed to be fairly normal.

The worship in the room was heavenly, raw, eclectic, and alternative all at once. I went to places that I'd never gone before. I met an awesome Father who had good gifts to give. He touched me with His hand in an indescribable way. The sermon was more like a testimony than a three point exegetical expose` to which I was accustomed. However, it was meaty and had many nuggets of gold. I knew somehow that I was getting an impartation of the Father's Heart rather than just talking about God as if He were a million light years away. Heaven was downloading His love, helping me experience the living God rather than just hearing a Greek lesson on love. Every sense of religion inside my spirit was about to leave. The pastor, John Arnott, announced that we needed to move our chairs and line up single file according to the taped lines on the carpet. He told us we were about to flow into ministry time, aka, "carpet time."

On the floor—that's where I met Jesus and His love for me! As we lined up, there was a ministry team that prayed for us. There was nothing hurried about this. They had plenty of time to minister to all of us. There was no manipulation. Most everyone "fell in the Spirit." There were "catchers" behind us to catch us if we fell, but not everyone fell. None of the ministry team pushed us in any way. I stood waiting, watching. Clearly, my time was coming. I could see the ministry team headed my way as more and more received a physical touch of His love. Then, "it" happened as I received prayer. The same sensation came over me that I experienced when God healed my foot (see Ch. 1). The Holy Spirit came into me from my head and flowed through me to the tips of my toes. It was an elation; light, airy, renewing. I was clearly born again—again. I found myself "swooned" in the Spirit, laying on a floor with thousands of others. I thought about getting up, but I couldn't. I just could not get off the floor. So, I quietly listened to the worship music and to God. He reminded me of an incident that occurred when I was in the seventh grade. I saw where insecurity had broken into my life while I was just a mere Junior Higher. I realized that Jesus wanted to heal that memory. In my memory, while I was being falsely accused, I saw Jesus healing me. For the first time, I was able to forgive my accusers. In retrospect, I see that Jesus was healing me in a deep place, what I call "inner healing" now. At the time, I didn't have a clue about it. Jesus was healing me in spirit, soul, and body, long before I had even been introduced to inner healing. Finally, after thirty minutes, I got off the floor. God is good!

The next night, I ran down for ministry with a shovel full of less reluctance, hoping to be first in line. David Ruis led us to the throne room of God during worship; Randy Clark spoke on the love of the Father. Suddenly, I got whacked again. I expected to hear new things from God, but I didn't count on what actually happened. There was an English speaking French Canadian who spent an hour with me as I lay on the floor. This girl prophesied everything in the world over me. She prayed over me, poured the Holy Spirit over me, spoke realities of the Kingdom into me, brought inner healing to me, allowed God to change me, and transform me into a better person!

Many may read this and wonder and judge with a critical mind. You might say, "Where is that in the Bible?" Surprise, it's in there! The power of God did a lot of unusual things as recorded in the Bible. Look at King Saul, Ezekiel, Jeremiah, Daniel, Saul/Paul, just to name a few. Moreover, I know this, "I was blind, but now I see!" While on that floor, I fell in love with the Father. I finally realized that He was good and wanted to bless me. He wanted to give me a future and a hope. I became a better father, husband, and pastor. I could hear His voice much clearer! I was hooked on Him and He was hooked on me.

WHILE ON THE FLOOR, I FELL IN LOVE WITH THE FATHER.

By the third night, I was on the ministry team, serving as a "catcher." I don't know why they let me help, but I had favor. By eleven o'clock, it was time for the ministry team to pray for one another. We got blasted. Literally, I was drunk. I could hardly walk. I couldn't find the bus to get us back to the hotel. Candy had to deal with a drunk husband for the first time in her life.

I should stop here! I probably shouldn't go on, but I have to. The Spirit of the Lord has given me freedom. When I say we were hooked on Him, I mean we needed Him to accomplish all that He needed to accomplish. To this day, seventeen years later, I look for Him like a junky would for drugs. He is the cocaine I feel every time I minister to someone. I like "to do the stuff" because it is fun, freeing, and

I feel like I'm flying! I know some people who are just now encountering more of the Holy Spirit and they describe it as "a ministry high." Back in the '70s and '80s, Christians coined the phrase, "high on Him." Even today, some get "high" when they are in God's presence. "Be not drunk with wine, but be filled with the Holy Spirit" (Eph. 5:18). Now I understand the implication! The correlation Paul is making is that drinking the Holy Spirit might cause inebriation. You may need a designated driver after leaving a meeting like that!

It was the real deal. I came home and started praying for people and they would just fall down. One guy fell down so hard that he bent the metal chair behind him and offended the religious spirit in a guy nearby. Granted, the guy was used to a more calm "religious service." That's what you call hitting two stones with one bird; i.e., Holy Spirit (dove).

More importantly, I prayed for my children! They were ages four, eleven, and thirteen. As soon as we came home from Toronto, I prayed for my oldest daughter and she felt the power of the Holy Spirit. She said, "Daddy, I feel something warm in my stomach; it feels good, but strange at the same time." Soon after, two of my children began prophesying. (We all hear from God now.) My four year old sang as she walked down the hallway of our home, "Pour out your Spirit, Lord. Pour out your Spirit."

Is it real? You're God blessed right, it's real! He is real and He wants to flood your life with His heart, His love! IT MAY NOT COME IN THE PACKAGE I HAVE DESCRIBED because the God of all creativity likes to do it in His way, His package! (Isa. 55:8-9) He wants to reveal, download, and change your heart from a stony heart to a heart of flesh (Ezek. 36:26). God is releasing you, the Elijah Generation, to carry the Father's heart, ministering in His love and power.

I visited Toronto several times and each time, the Holy Spirit visited me in power and in love. In November 1995, we took our two oldest children to a healing conference held by Toronto Fellowship, led by Mahesh Chavda. Our son was sitting with us about thirty rows back from the stage and Mahesh had a "word of knowledge" about chronic fatigue syndrome. He stood up, along with a few others and Mahesh prayed for them. Our son was healed from Epstein Barr Syndrome and the fevers and symptoms that had consistently plagued him since he was four years old.

GOD IS RELEASING YOU, THE ELIJAH GENERATION, TO CARRY THE FATHER'S HEART, MINISTERING IN HIS LOVE AND POWER.

There were thousands of healings just like this, but this is just the beginning. My heart resonates with Bob Jones from Morning Star when he explains how the "Outpouring of Toronto" was the river that only went up to your ankles (Ezek. 47). The Brownsville Revival was the river that went up to our knees. There were so many who were saved during that revival. What is coming next is the river that comes over our heads. It can't be contained. This is the Third Great Awakening, which my friend, Danny Steyne, is igniting. This is what we are getting ready for. Prepare the way!

Receiving the Father's Blessing

Many prophetic words have been given to my wife and me over the years about the Father's Heart and how we carry

His heart as a Mom and Pop. Malachi 4:5-6 has been drummed in us so many times. For years, whenever we received prophetic prayer ministry, there was an obvious theme of the Father's Heart being released through us. The prophecies, time and time again, spoke of the many young people who would be drawn to us, sent by the Lord. "Turning the hearts of the children back to the Father" has been our MO for some time now. That is what we do! One of the first times we were made aware of this was in a meeting in 1995 with John Paul Jackson. He called us out of the audience of about 700 people in Atlanta and said we had the Father's Heart. That word so moved us! It shook us, spirit, soul and body! It even precipitated a move to plant another church in a new location. On a side note, we are involved in planting more churches in Africa some seventeen years later! The takeaway is that we had the Father's Heart. I really didn't have full revelation of what that meant, but I would soon grow in understanding.

Giving away the Father's Heart
Love in Peru

During a heavy missions season of my life, we found ourselves going to Peru quite a bit. I was blessed to be with Johnny Enlow on a number of occasions for a period of about five years during the early 2000s. It was a beautiful training period for God to do a number of things in my heart. The Lord had really imparted the Father's Heart in me and I truly just wanted to set others free by His Spirit. On one of our journeys to Peru, God was really stirring the waters.

Of course, there were language barriers! Having taken French in high school, Greek in college, and Hebrew in seminary, there was quite a collision of files on my hard drive.

And, if I might say, the process of downloading Spanish on top of that was getting a bit tricky. The linguistic area of my brain could take only a few more imprints and I was done. So, I found myself going to Spanish speaking countries and I needed to learn some basics. Not to be out done by the barriers while ministering to people, I had developed a "cheat sheet" that I could rely on. However, there is a huge difference between the spoken language and the written word as I was soon to find.

Typically, Johnny would preach and the ministry team would either give prophetic words from the pulpit, with Johnny's interpretation, or we would just "lay hands on" the expectant crowd. One night in Lima was "hot" with the Father's Heart and His touch. All I wanted to do was pray for people and I was free to do it. Thankfully, Johnny led us to pray for people. My guns were cocked and ready to go. I pulled out my cheat sheet and I was ready to pray "the heart of the Father"—joy, love, and many other choice words I had learned from Johnny earlier. Why, I was a walking lexicon for praying for others in Spanish; at least, so I thought.

"Mas amore, mas amore," I prayed over person after person. I was praying, "more love, more love." One by one, they just fell out in the Spirit. "Wow," I thought, "God is really doing a lot here tonight." I knew the power of God was on me. In fact, God was really ministering around the room.

Afterwards, we ate our usual late night meal of chicken and rice. We were discussing and processing all that God did that night, when the dessert came. I asked politely, "What is it?" I distinctly heard the word, "amore." I thought, "What kind of dessert would be called 'love'?" After some investigation, I found out that it's spelled a lot like "love" and even pronounced like it, but just the inflection in one's voice determines the difference. So, you might be saying "love," or you might be saying, "jello." "JELLO!" I exclaimed. Did I pray for people to become like jello, or did I pray for more of Papa's love? I turned to Johnny and asked, "Did I ask God to turn them into jello?" That's why they fell over one by one when I prayed for them. They became like jello!

We laughed and laughed!! Be careful what you ask for! However, God was doing some incredible things that night. Relationships were renewed, people were healed, and the evidence of the love of the Father was all over the room. It's amazing how Papa works in spite of our simple efforts. One woman I prayed over for twenty minutes or so got back together with her husband. Awesome!

The Father's Heart
"Break our hearts with what breaks yours!"

Yeah, we were young and foolish when we prayed that prayer. It is a good prayer, but we didn't know what that might look like. God had to break our hearts in order for us to carry all that He wanted for us! Going to the cross is only for a brief moment compared to His supernatural loving-kindness that dwells forever. Our desire was "...to know His power, together with all the saints, to grasp how wide and long and high and deep is the love of Christ, and to know this love that surpasses knowledge..." (Eph. 3:18-19). Sometimes our knowledge and presuppositions have to get out of the way for God to work. Our religion, control, and theological systems have to step aside for us to begin to truly comprehend His love. We really had to die to self, take up our cross, and follow Him (Matt. 16:24).

Integrity requires me to put in the bad with the good. Listen, everyone that I prayed for didn't get healed. John

Wimber said to pray for 1000 people; again, commit to pray for 1000 people for healing and someone will get healed. You'll learn how to do it along the way. Your percentages will go up. You'll begin to know your gifts and strengths. While there are many who didn't get healed, I rejoice in the ones who *were healed*. In fact, the more inner healing I received personally, the more healings I saw!

Candy and I did go through the "dark night of the soul." I knew something huge was going to happen at the turn of the century and it did. We were turned inside out. Our marriage was tested, our church closed down, we both had to get "regular jobs," we were tested in our family, questions of faith abounded, and we were arrested at the core of our being.

We had gone after inner healing. Jerry and Denise Basel, whose ministry is called, of course, "The Father's Heart," facilitated an Elijah House Prayer Counseling Course by John and Paula Sandford. At least half of 1998 was devoted to this study and inner healing time. God was really up to something by touching all the parts of our hearts that needed changing and realignment.

Finally, in the year 2000, the wheels of the wagon fell off. We were done! I'm so thankful to this day that Jerry and Denise Basel were there to pick up the pieces of our lives and extricate all the bitterness and anger that had been stored up in my heart. I was deeply angry at Candy, the church, and even God. Praise God for His infinite mercy and grace. Yes, His mercy, for not giving me what I deserve, and His grace, for giving more of His Love than I can think or imagine.

"Oh, the depth of the riches of the wisdom and knowledge of God! How unsearchable His judgments and His paths beyond tracing out! Who has known the mind of the Lord? Or who has been His counselor? Who has ever given to God that God should repay Him? For from Him and through Him and to Him are all things. To Him be the glory forever! Amen" (Rom. 11: 33-36).

The enemy desired to keep us bitter and full of pride. He had a vested interest. Though we all take full responsibility for our actions, the enemy is always right there to tear us down. Notice that Sanballat was there as Nehemiah was rebuilding the wall around Jerusalem. The Assyrian governor did not want the wall rebuilt, so he resisted the man of God. When Jesus resisted the Pharisees regarding their religious practices, the establishment fatally opposed Jesus to protect their vested interest. Demetrius attacked Paul after a groundswell of Christians stopped buying idols from the silversmith. Demetrius protected his vested interest. When you come against the territory of the enemy and attack the gates of Hades with your keys to the Kingdom, then guess what, the enemy will not roll over and play dead. He has a vested interest in you and all that you are doing. However, prayer is the tool that keeps him at bay. Prayer is the gateway to life, relationship, and healing!

The Lord has healed us! Inner healing is the gateway to physical healing. Bitterness is the result of a pride that has not been broken. Jesus did say, "For whoever wants to save his life will lose it, but whoever loses his life for me will find it" (Matt. 16:25). There is a brokenness for sure, a cross to carry, a death to self; HOWEVER, WE CAN'T LIVE THERE! We live in the resurrection of His glory. Too many live in the shadow of the cross! Go ahead and die, and get over it. The easiest thing in the world for God to do is bring death to pride and selfish ambition. You, however, are to live in His resurrection power and stop stomping around the pig's trough. It's time for us to wash off the muck and the mire, and go back to Papa. He has a robe, a crown, a ring, and a fatted calf as He waits for His sons and daughters to come home!

Repent??? Yes, but not in the manner you may think. We repent from not just "sin," but from religion, impotence, pride, bitterness, and our alliance with the anti-Christ! Yes, every time you disdain someone flowing in the anointing of the Holy Spirit, you have identified with the anti-Christ spirit and mirrored the image of the enemy, the father of lies. Each time you ridicule someone who speaks in tongues, or when you deny the power of God, or healing, or if you have thought, "God doesn't work that way today," you have agreed with the enemy and empowered his work. If you have even thought, "God wouldn't work that way for me," you have partaken from the rich morsels of the anti-Christ's table. See, "Christ" means "Anointed One." It isn't Jesus' last name. His name is the Anointed One! To deny His power in any way is to deny Christ! Repent, and be a part of the generation that brings in the Christ rather than joining the work of the anti-Christ. What if the anti-Christ, who many are looking for before Christ returns, is in your own back yard, perpetrating "doctrine" rather than the "anointing?" Something to think about, isn't it?

Doctrine is not a substitute for a love affair. Doctrine may give us definition and understanding, but it also gives us a sense of superiority. To purport doctrine over the power of God—Christ—we are, in essence, saying that our religion is more important than Jesus Christ! That's why doctrine can be so destructive. If you use doctrine to exclude others from your culture and define your superiority, it is a form of racism, which in turn, is the seedbed for genocide and ethnic cleansing. Some people I've met who are doctrinally opposed to the anointing of Jesus in this hour and opposed to the radical expressions of His sons and daughters are very toxic. I see and feel the hatred in their countenance.

DOCTRINE IS NOT A SUBSTITUTE FOR A LOVE AFFAIR.

The teachings of the Bible can be renewed over and over in every generation. Light can come from the Word when it witnesses to what God is doing in the present hour. The Word complements what God is doing today. We would rather focus on living a life that does align with His Word. When we do that, two things happen. One is that the Godhead becomes Father, Son, and Holy Spirit instead of Father, Son, and Holy Bible. Secondly, our doctrine may shift in understanding to what God is doing rather than designing rigid structures that are impenetrable by any other belief system and which foster exclusiveness and judgment.

WHAT HAPPENED TO LOVE? I had been a preacher for fifteen years and been married about that long before I knew love or Jesus Christ! I remember pondering many times, "What is love?" and "How do I get it?" Is it controlled by the will and not by my emotions as compartmentalized religion taught me? This led me to become very controlling. I controlled my mind and my emotions. I was in complete control! No, actually, I was out of control! Yet, in 1994, Jesus saved me again and it has been a love affair ever since.

HIS LOVE TRANSFORMS.
HIS LOVE RAINS UPON US WITH MERCY AND
    GRACE.

HE WANTS TO BLESS US.

HE WANTS US TO HAVE ABUNDANT LIFE.

HE HAS A FUTURE AND A HOPE FOR US.

HE HAS BREATHED UPON US SONSHIP!

HE HAS DESTINY AND DIRECTION. HE HAS A
FUTURE AND A HOPE!

HIS LOVE GIVES AND GIVES!

HE WANTS YOU TO HAVE AN EPIC JOURNEY.

HE WANTS YOU TO KNOW WHAT HE IS
THINKING.

HE WANTS YOU TO HAVE KINGDOM AUTHORITY.

HE WANTS YOU TO HEAR HIS VOICE.

HE WANTS YOU TO DECLARE HEALING OVER
OTHERS' LIVES.

HE WANTS YOU TO DREAM BIG DREAMS!

God is love. He is your Wonderful Counselor, your
Everlasting Father who never leaves you nor forsakes you
(Isa. 9:6). He wants to know you on a personal and emotional
basis. He is the Father Himself who tenderly loves you (John
16:27). His unfailing love for you will never be shaken (Isa.
54:10). Jesus is the Binder of broken hearts, the Comforter
for all who mourn, the One who gives beauty in exchange for
ashes, gladness for mourning and praise for despair (Isa. 61:
1-3).

Where are the fathers? Where are the fathers who will
turn the hearts of the children back to the Father? Paul said
even in his day that there weren't many fathers (1 Cor. 4:15).
There are some here today who have suffered to say,

LET THIS ELIJAH GENERATION COME FORTH
NOW! IN JESUS'—THE ANNOINTED ONE'S NAME!
LET US PREPARE THE WAY FOR JESUS' RETURN
AND ESTABLISH HIS KINGDOM!

Just a thought to shake an eschatological view: What if Jesus' return is NOW! What if His Kingdom is NOW! What if all that you have been waiting for, all that is in your theological view, whereby, having a long list of prerequisites before Christ can return, are really mostly attainable now? "Let your Kingdom come, your will be done on earth as it is in heaven [NOW]." Life as we know it would be quite powerful, wouldn't it? I've got good news—life is great! It's not that I've

> ...already obtained all this, or have already been made perfect, but I press on to take hold of that for which Christ Jesus took hold of me...I press on
> toward the goal to win the prize for which God has called me heavenward in Christ. (Phil. 3:12, 14)

The prize in life is to be in Him all the time! He is the prize! I don't just have a heaven perspective; heaven is in me and I am in heaven. I plan to continue living this heavenward life! GOOD NEWS: The bad news was wrong. Now, that is a gospel I can live with!

The Father's Heart has been costly! We've spent our entire lives seeking the truth about God. We've spent a bunch of money to find out: God, who are You and what are You doing? We've asked, "Can we do the things that Jesus did and are they real today?" Did we find Him? Not exactly, He found us and He is so good! God is so good! He is the author of good! (Gen. 1) He wants to bless you and keep you. We have paid a price so that many may know Him, walk in His Presence, and do the things that Jesus did. Prepare the Way!

4

1000 HEALINGS

Tanzania, Africa. My first solo mission trip with a team traveling with me. Most of the time, we preach Jesus and His Kingdom and then see God work. It is always incredible. Always!

On the island of Zanzibar, God did some incredible things. At one church, everyone was taught to hear God's voice; about fifteen people were healed of a variety of sicknesses and diseases. Our faith was built up and we were ready to go! After three days of preaching and doing the Kingdom stuff, we were now ready to minister to some United States missionaries. It was fun.

One particular night was filled with worship. We had a great night in the Lord. God's presence and power were amazing as He released healing—several inner healings and a physical healing. I only differentiate so that you may understand that God heals in a variety of ways. We are to love God with all parts of our being: spirit, soul, and body (1 Thess. 5:23). Later, I will discuss some of the intricacies of inner healing, but for now, notice how a spirit of unforgiveness may be linked to a physical ailment. For example, Jesus modeled this link when He healed the paralytic saying, "Your sins are forgiven" and He then healed him (Matt. 9:1-8). I've noticed many times how unforgiveness and judgments are linked to bone problems. This was the case that night in Tanzania.

Hazel was a missionary in her mid-to-late forties who was worshiping with us. She had participated in the presence of the Lord by giving several words and a short teaching. Hazel had even witnessed a powerful healing with one of the younger guys. She saw how Jesus transformed and redirected this young computer techie. Jesus had shown up in Mark's memory and healed a situation that had held him captive for years. Mark believed that Jesus didn't like him because of an incident from his high school days. Jesus washed away all his sins, bitterness, and hatred toward God! "Well, that's good for a twenty year old, but I'm farther along than that," Hazel must have thought. "I don't have issues like that; I've been a missionary for twenty years. Surely I've forgiven everyone in my life."

Just as we were finishing with Mark, Hazel came to me and asked me to pray with her regarding her knee. It had been giving her problems with pain and general flexibility. We began to pray and after a few moments, Hazel began to cry. I asked her, "Do you have anyone you need to forgive?" She was silent. I continued to pray the love of the Father over her. I asked Jesus to show her where there might be a link to her physical problems. I asked her, "Has Jesus shown you anything?" Again, silence—other than a few ST's (snot and tears). Hazel then began to cry harder and said, "I vowed I would never mention his name again." "Who?" I asked cleverly! Silence, once more. I then encouraged her, with

54

complete honor, to reveal the person's name. I honored her silence, but gently coaxed her to do what I saw the Heavenly Father doing. I saw Papa wanting to do what He does best, bring healing. Her lips began to quiver and I heard a shaky voice declare, "I can't say his name." This went on for about five long minutes. After some further gentle coaxing and half a box of Kleenex, she finally said, "Jack. Jack is his name." The room was again deafening, but this time with loud weeping and moaning. She cried, "I forgive Jack; I forgive him!" Little did she know, that was my next question. "Can you forgive him?" I guess the Holy Spirit was a step ahead of me! (Ya think?)

Hazel forgave Jack. I led her in prayers of repentance of judgments she had made toward Jack. She renounced the spirit of bitterness and judgment in the name of Jesus. We prayed blessings over her and filled her with good words and the Holy Spirit. I then said, "Oh yeah, Kingdom of God come to her knee! Be healed in Jesus' name." I asked about her knee. She said it felt better and it felt warm. "Is the pain gone?" "Yes!" she exclaimed. "Jump." She did and the rest is history. She was healed. God healed her—spirit, soul, and body! About a year later, I heard she was at the church we then attended in the States and she was doing well. Praise God!

God heals in many ways. He desires to heal the whole person. I have found people of two extremes. Either they believe that God is spiritual, so He only does spiritual things and He's not too concerned about our physical needs. They might say, "You know, He has given us doctors to heal the sick and has given us a sound mind to make good decisions via strong Biblical principles." Hence, they pray: "Lord, give wisdom to the doctors and the nurses in this operation," never asking God to just simply heal the person. They also pray on big decisions, "You've given us a sound mind, now give us wisdom on what house to buy," taking the intimate and personal God out of the equation. The other extreme is the Christian who believes in healing, but not inner healing. "Christ did everything at the cross and that's all we need. His blood accomplished everything and cancelled sin, so we don't need to go back and revisit any of our past." Well, my response is, "How is that working out for you?" I mean that seriously. Empirically, I see that people, Christians—my brothers and sisters—are still carrying STUFF! We all know STUFF HAPPENS! And it really gets messy!

GOD HEALS IN MANY WAYS. HE DESIRES TO HEAL THE WHOLE PERSON.

"I'm fine!" I hear that too often. Jesus has done it all; I agree, but you have to let Him have it all. He has chosen the church to get rid of the self-inflicting stuff. Then the church can do the Kingdom stuff with Jesus. "His intent was that now through the church, His manifold wisdom (grace and power) should be known to the rulers and authorities in the heavenlies…" (Eph. 3:7-13). Most people who say they are just fine are really saying something like this:

I'm Fine…
Freaked Out
Insecure
Neurotic
Emotional
(From the movie, *The Italian Job*)

What do you do with Christians who have problems? Send them to a doctor? Well, sometimes; but I have found Dr. Jesus! Rather than sending Christians to humanistic counselors and psychiatrists, Jesus has the answer. Try implementing the power of Jesus' blood to the specific wound before throwing the little lambs to the wolves. When lambs become lions, we eat the wolves. People in our churches have dire needs from dysfunction to depression, from bi-polar to bi-partners, and many of these issues can be healed. Throwing a twenty-minute Bible history lesson once a week will not transform these people. Jesus has the answer and the answer is different every time! There are no secret formulas, just Jesus. The beauty is that He did resurrect and I have good news: He is a tangible, imparting, manifesting person in our midst today. He wants to do what he does best—minister through us by way of His Holy Spirit. I WANT THAT!

We all need healing. Candy and I have facilitated over 1000 inner healing sessions. We have prayed with a wanting brother or sister for over two or three hours, literally hundreds of times. I counted one time that we have nearly a year of our lives invested in facilitating inner healings with people and training others how to do it. We have trained other churches both in the States and abroad. We now have an ongoing part of our ministry (Lifegate) for the healing of the spirit, soul, and body. We have wonderful trained prayer ministers who work with us to free the captive and release the prisoner from darkness (Isa. 61:1). Our ministry hosts the healing power of Jesus at least three to six times a week. We have documented proof and testimonies that these healings are real. Thousands, literally, thousands have been healed!!!! All glory to God! Praise be to God!

With the exception of a very small number out of a thousand (maybe a handful), each person leaves their prayer encounter with a sincere sense of freedom, reconciliation with the Father, and burdens lifted. The most common response at the end of a prayer session is, "I feel light; I feel good." We have so many spiritual children as a result of this powerful, healing prayer ministry. They share their testimony and bring back others to experience a similar freedom. If people weren't being healed, they wouldn't tell their friends. We don't know where all they come from, but every week, they come! God is breathing on inner healing ministry and anyone can do it. We now have a team of prayer leaders at Lifegate who are trained to take back what the enemy has stolen. Some have studied further, accumulating more tools and keys of ministry, including: Sozo, Theophostics, Listening Prayer, Spirit Ministry, and Heart Sync, to name a few. Praise God for these warriors!

As mentioned before, Candy and I were trained by Elijah House in 1998. We later were trained in Sozo, a ministry of Bethel Church, Redding, CA. We received hands-on Sozo training by Andy Reese, Franklin, TN, who carries Papa's heart and releases Sozo ministry helps through Freedom Prayer (www.freedomprayer.org).

Sozo is the Greek word Jesus used many times in the context of salvation, deliverance, and healing. Seemingly, the inference of these meanings are interchangeable and may cross over from time to time by the context of the Scriptures. However, Jesus didn't have a problem using the same word for the purpose at hand, intermingling these definitions into one thought. Hence, when one is saved, he is delivered, or healed. Congruently, when one is healed, salvation and deliverance usually occurs. Or, when one is delivered, he is healed and saved. For example, when Jesus healed the paralytic (Mark 2:1-12), He said, "Son, your sins are forgiven." Then He talked of salvation: "Which is easier to say to the paralytic, 'Your sins are forgiven or to say, 'Get up, take up your mat and walk'?" In many other passages, deliverance and healing seem to work simultaneously (see Matt. 9:32-33).

While there is always a connection to the three definitions, all three are not always performed at one time. Yes, there can be a healing without deliverance. So you can have one without the other. However, John Sandford says that prayer ministry is "evangelizing the heart!" You are always to bring more deliverance and freedom to the soul of man. This is a quick, supernatural work of transformation and sanctification that takes place in a matter of a couple of hours! Many times, the demonic is at work. It's usually very subtle, but we deal with that, too.

The result: healing! In every classical sense of the word—to make or become whole! Papa comes to the complete man and makes him whole. It is His "desire to make us whole in every way: spirit, soul, and body (1 Thess. 5:23). He saves us, delivers us, and heals us. He restores the "paradise lost." That which the enemy has stolen from the Garden of Eden is reconciled through Jesus Christ. We are made whole by being clothed with Christ, one piece of clothing at a time. Through Jesus, the one being healed is changed by destroying lies the enemy implanted, reconciling the relationship with Papa via encounters with truth, and healing the wounds of the broken man. I've seen this happen over and over again! We now call our Sozo ministry *LifeChanges* because it has evolved, using a number of different tools to "undo the works of the enemy" (1 John 3:8b).

In John 10:10, Jesus says that "the thief comes only to steal, kill, and destroy; I have come that they may have life, and have it to the full." *LifeChanges* is an inner healing ministry with the focused intent of helping individuals gain freedom from the effects of wounding and sin. Its purpose is to set the captives free (Isa. 61). In John 8:32, we learn that if we hold to Jesus' teachings, we will "...know the truth and the truth will set us free." Where the enemy has planted his lies in us, God wants to take those lies and exchange them for *His truth* so we may walk in wholeness and freedom. We are then able to walk in our true identity as sons and daughters of a loving, mighty Father.

Holy Spirit is the greatest teacher of all and continues to bring new understanding to the path of inner healing. Through the experience of praying for numerous people over the years, Holy Spirit has imparted new insights and truths which have been incorporated into inner healing ministry.

I recall some of the early Patristic Fathers of the first and second centuries having a process of salvation that actually got the job done. They would accept people's confessions of faith, get them baptized, delivered and healed; and then baptize them in the Holy Spirit. I actually tried this in May 2011 in Sierra Leone, Africa. There was a young church plant, about six weeks old. Many wanted to be baptized, so we accepted their confession, delivered all of them from demons and tormenting spirits, healed (or sozoed) them, and then baptized them in the Holy Spirit; then they all spoke in tongues. None of them had ever done any of this. This had to be a sovereign work of God! We then drove and walked about ten miles to baptize them in two feet of water. This was so much like the book of Acts. Oh, yeah, by the way, about twenty were healed of various diseases and physical maladies!

Why not get it done all at once! What is holding back the church from healing? Whether you trace it back to 18th century theology, from the demythologizing of the Bible by Rudolph Bultmann, to William Barclay, to a post-modern church, the devil has neutralized the church to be lukewarm at all costs. The best way to become inoculated from anything is to take small doses of the real item and over time, you will build up a resistance to it. The church has inoculated us to the real thing, maybe not out of maliciousness, but perhaps out of ignorance.

It is time, not for a paradigm shift, but a quantum leap! It is time for the church to take one giant step forward. The enemy wants us to be pathetic individuals, whining for more milk. He wants us to believe that no one can even become demon possessed today. The very root of the cessationist movement is the lie that we don't need the Holy Spirit gifts; therefore, there is no need, nor power, to kick the devil out of people. Jesus taunted the Pharisees by saying that satan can't drive out satan! And a kingdom can't be divided by itself! (Mark 3:23) Could it be that the well-known technique of deliverance used by Jesus and continued after Jesus' resurrection for centuries was set off to the side by satan himself? Wouldn't it be accurate for the father of lies to trick the church into believing there is no need for healing, there is no need for deliverance, there is no need for power?

Wake up, oh sleepy church, keep your nice buildings, youth programs, videos, and loud speakers. Let's keep your seeker-sensitive Sunday morning window dressing. But somewhere, we have to wake up and aspire for *more*: "You know that He appeared so that He might take away our sins...the reason the Son of God appeared was to destroy the devil's work" (1 John 3: 5,8). There is a war! Be the lion!

Healing! What does it look like? HEALING, SALVATION, and DELIVERANCE FROM THE TOR-MENTOR. Jesus heals spirit, soul, and body. It seems you were created for this! Jump on in, the water is fine. It is fun to be apart of this Elijah Generation doing the "stuff!"

"Don't make me leave; I like this body!"

"As you go, preach this message: 'The Kingdom of heaven is near.' Heal the sick, raise the dead, cleanse those who have leprosy, drive out demons. Freely you have received, freely give" (Matt. 10: 7-8).

Jesus is the great healer! Jehovah Rophe (the healer) is His name. If Holy Spirit is now in us and we are His sons, should we not look at His face and become healed, become a healer? As we received, we so give.

Several years ago, Jay, Jeff and I went on a mission trip to India. We knew we were going there to preach the gospel, the good news of Jesus Christ and His Kingdom. We were also going to scope the land in order to, perhaps, do more work there and support some local orphanages and churches. After flying to Mumbai, then to Chennai, taking a six hour train ride to Hyderabad, and a two hour taxi ride near Narasaraopet, we arrived less than perky at 2:00 a.m. in the morning. I might say Sunday morning, for we had "junior" church for about 100 kids the next morning at 8:00 a.m. For ten days straight, we had preaching, teaching, prayer times, healings, and worship every night and sometimes during the day. We held a pastors conference on the first Monday and Tuesday. Jay had the brilliant idea to start out by washing the feet of the pastors. It was a blessed time and God moved among the men and women at that conference. Many words of prophecy were spoken and a few got healed.

After that, every night was an incredible experience. The three of us would rotate preaching and many times, the whole village was saved and many were healed. Edwin, the local missionary, kept count of the healings; it was in the hundreds. I recall one lady who had bled for ten years who was healed and she told her family about this Jesus. The next night, she brought her family to the meeting and they got saved. We questioned the integrity of some of the miracles or healings because of cultural characteristics. Even as I report to you the fact that God healed many, for we could see it in their faces, I'm sure there were some who claimed their healing because of who we are—Americans with huge resources of money. Yet, the Lord was opening India to us as if the New Testament itself was being read aloud to us. There was no denying the work of His supernatural hand!

WHEREVER WE WERE THE WEAKEST, WE WERE STRONG. CHRIST MADE US STRONG.

Many miracles, signs, and wonders were accounted for on this trip. What I am about to share is an accurate account of what we saw and heard. Though the trip was the hardest trip I've ever been on, it was one of the most glorious. Wherever we were the weakest, we were strong. Christ made us strong.

On one particular night, it was my time to preach and by this time Edwin, our interpreter, was becoming hoarse since this was about the eighth or ninth night he translated for us. The anointing was building and the three amigos had sung the only song we knew, "Open the Eyes of My Heart." I had put the words to the song in my backpack right before leaving the States, thinking we might need them. Well, in every village, they asked us to sing. So, we sang this song which came to be a ritual as we traveled from village to village. Fortunately, there were no dogs in this village to howl at our sound. Now, it was my time to preach. I preached a good salvation message. I'm sure I threw in a little D. James Kennedy stuff from "Evangelism Explosion." We offered the invitation as usual, expecting many to come to Christ. None came. We preached a little more and still none. We looked at each other. I didn't want to browbeat anyone, but the other villages were so easy. What happened to these people? They were supposed to respond on cue, weren't they?

We brought the evening to an end and asked if anyone wanted prayer. No one ever turns that down and I was right! All that we could see came to the front for prayer. They were all ladies and were the only ones in the front. I know in many churches or gatherings in other countries, the men and women separate. The women and children wanted prayer. We simply said, "Jesus come" and He came!

What an awkward moment! Yet, many times God will use those awkward moments to reveal His glory! You see, we had gone to the uttermost parts of the earth, carrying the message of the Kingdom. We had preached the Gospel and now were waiting for a response. If God didn't show up, we'd had it; this was going to be a total failure. We knew there was no manipulation taking place. God had to do something or we were toast. So, I began praying. Jay and Jeff were evenly dispersed throughout the crowd. I prayed for a young girl and she immediately fell to the ground. I thought to myself, "This is good—now we're getting somewhere; people will see this and then come to Christ." Ha, not yet.

The young girl fell to the ground, but she began writhing, her body twisting back and forth, slithering like a snake. Everyone stood back as if they knew what she might do. She became a spectacle, so Jay and several other pastors took her to the back and cast out the demon. Jay later told me there were several demons and it took a few minutes. I continued praying for people and they said they were healed. We had them point to the pain in their bodies and our interpreters would ask them if they were better. They always said yes. You could see the sheer delight, joy, and glory of the Lord on their face! This was not of man, but of God.

Jay came back with the young girl. She was smiling; her countenance had completely changed. She had been delivered. I'm not sure which was most noticeable: the joy that exuded from this girl's face or the shock on the crowd's faces. Later, we found out the young woman had been involved in witchcraft (of course), Hindu idol worship, and satanic ritual. But all that was gone! The people were awestruck. Suddenly, there was a shakeup in the crowd. The men who were standing on the outskirts quickly became a part of the mix. They wanted prayer. We prayed for hours as many were delivered, healed, and set free.

Picture this dramatic downdraft of the Holy Spirit:

- The young woman, full of demons, was set free.
- Men crowded in, wanting prayer and some of this Jesus.
- I prayed for a little boy on crutches. He'd had polio all his life and even had bandages on his knees where he'd fallen. This innocent, beautiful child lay down his crutches and walked!

Meanwhile, Jeff had been praying for people during this time. He prayed for one and delivered her. We heard the 75-year-old lady scream at the top of her voice:

"DON'T MAKE ME LEAVE; I LIKE THIS BODY!"

We laughed about it later, but it was pretty intense at the time. Can't you climb in the minds of these people? Don't you think they were saying something like, "Who are these guys? Even the spirits obey their voice in the name of Jesus!" (Mark 1:27)

Then Jay received a "word of knowledge" and he just stood up on a table in the middle of the crowd and said, "You see this girl who just got delivered? You have a choice tonight. You can have the joy you see in her and choose Jesus, or you can go home and be tormented by the nightmares you've had for years!"

ALL HEAVEN BROKE LOOSE! Hundreds came to know Jesus that night! Men and women accepted Jesus. The beauty was that we were traveling with pastors from village to village and these pastors could shepherd these new believers into the Kingdom! It wasn't just a crusade that would fizzle out after we left. Praise God!

I learned a lot that night! Wow, a power encounter just like Elijah!

God likes that stuff. Bill Johnson says that God likes to show up and show off. I think He likes to show off His sons and daughters, too. He likes to show off the crazy, risk-taking faith in these three guys from the States. I could finish now and tell you that God is calling you to do the stuff, but it doesn't stop here.

The three of us, on our one day off, went sight-seeing at

a dam a few miles from Narasaraopet. Due to a drought, the lake behind the Nagarjunasagar Dam was nearly empty. This was a large dam, in fact the largest masonry dam of its time. The three of us prayed and made declarations over the lake and the nation. In faith, we decreed that God was going to raise the level of the water in the dam just as He was going to raise the spiritual level in the country of India. We prayed for an hour or more and soon left. Interestingly enough, we later went through a nearby city and our lives were nearly threatened as our taxis landed right in the middle of a demonstration between Muslims and Hindus. Of course, we had on shirts with "Team Jesus" printed in big bold letters! We escaped to safety and continued on our way. About three weeks after we left the country, Edwin told us that the water in the lake had suddenly raised about 100 meters. "What?!" We couldn't believe it. Edwin conveyed the news report of three guys from America who went to the lake and prayed and the lake filled with water! That was hard to swallow! In fact, it was too hard to believe that the lake rose 100 meters! We all doubted the legitimacy of the story until three years later when Jay was back in India on another journey. While there, he asked some other pastors if they'd heard anything about a lake miraculously raising its water level by 100 meters. They replied, "Oh yes, it was in all the papers. No one could explain it; yeah, three men from the States were here and prayed. Why do you ask?" Jay said, "I was one of the pastors who prayed over that lake." Not only did Jay receive favor on that trip, but now I can tell this story knowing that many witnesses attest to the truth of this event.

By the way, during our last Sunday in India, I had the honor of baptizing a Muslim for the first time. Back in the States on that very Sunday, my future daughter-in-law, who was Muslim, had a miraculous supernatural Jesus encounter and accepted Him as Savior.

You might think this happens every day. You're pretty close. I think it did for Elijah, and for Jesus. Now it can happen to you!

A quote by Teilhard de Chardin, "You are not a human being in search of a spiritual experience. You are a spiritual being immersed in a human experience,"[1] has been rephrased and popularized by Bill Johnson and others. Yet, I like to put it like this, "We aren't natural beings having a supernatural experience, but we are supernatural beings, naturally."

You are a lamb becoming a lion. God can and will use you!

A Chicken Named Sozo

Again, *sozo* is more than just deliverance, but on this one occasion, God delivered a young girl from demons. Four of us were on a mission trip to Sierra Leone, Africa, in the Spring of 2011. After several other God encounters on the trip, we had a pastors' conference. I knew many of the pastors from my previous trips. However, during this meeting we were going into areas we'd never gone before. We were teaching on spiritual authority and warfare.

You have heard of *paraprosdokians*, perhaps—certain little familiar quips that have a certain funny twist to them, such as: "Where there is a will, I want to be in it." There's one that might be apropos: "To be sure of hitting the target, shoot first and call whatever you hit the target." So we knew we were supposed to talk about spiritual warfare, but I didn't really know the target. I wasn't prepared for what was about to occur; or was I?

After discussing at length how to cast out a demon and

teaching on the Kingdom of God, a pastor brought two children up front and asked us to pray for them "for they had a demon." Even though he spoke in Krio, I understood what he was saying. I appreciate Justus, a lead pastor, translating for me; it gave me a little more time to respond.

Abraham was a little three year old who, I later learned, had been thrashing on the floor earlier that morning. He was in my bead of sight when Elizabeth caught my eye. She was a thirteen year old who seemed rather normal. I'm glad our team was standing behind me because I wasn't prepared for the "target." Elizabeth immediately fell to the floor, only to be cushioned by the arms of our team on the way down. As she lay writhing and twisting on the floor, the atmosphere in the room changed. The pastors sat calmly as if to say, "This happens all the time!" Moses, our indigenous missionary in Sierra Leone and Liberia, was on top of it immediately, commanding, "I cast you out in the name of Jesus!" Of course, it's not in the words, but in the power, so sometimes we have to go a step further.

I said, "Papa, what do you want to do here?" He showed me that Elizabeth had a spirit of "attention," so I cast that out and got a bit perturbed at the devil because he was getting a lot of attention. I didn't yell or jump or shout, but asked again, "Jesus, what are you up to?" He showed me she had several cuttings. I discerned that the cuts occurred during some kind of ritual. I went to every one of those cuts and denounced what the devil had done through witchcraft; I denounced the incantations that had been said over Elizabeth. I spoke the name of Jesus over her spirit, soul and body. Meanwhile, the team was praying for her and Moses was still declaring and releasing Kingdom authority over her.

As the team continued to pray for Elizabeth, I turned to

pray for Abraham. I thought we might as well heal two people at once. Sure enough, I cast out the demon from Abraham and simultaneously, Elizabeth got up from the floor. Both felt better. Abraham was a bit embarrassed, but he was obviously not throwing himself on the floor and Elizabeth had a warm glow about her. She seemed to receive about all the peace and joy one could encounter at one time. Elizabeth had been set free! Delivered! Her heart saved! Healed! In a nutshell, she'd fulfilled the definition of *sozo*.

By no means is this a typical inner healing session! This is just to demonstrate God's love in Africa, and, yes, He does heal! Elizabeth, naturally, stayed close to us the rest of the day. She drew quite close to one of our team members, Mary Elizabeth! They hit it off with one another, having the same name, and Mary Elizabeth was instrumental in Elizabeth's deliverance. Elizabeth was continually thankful that we had reached out to her and prayed for her. Later that day, we learned that she had been in a secret society which is quite common in Africa. To enter a secret society, one must make a blood covenant. Girls have to be circumcised to enter and guys are cut on the lower part of their backs. Demons are assigned to prevent them from leaving the society. Elizabeth's demon didn't want to let go of her, but it had to!

Finally, it was the end of a long day and we made our way to our rooms. I had just laid down when I heard a knock on my door at 11:00. It was Elizabeth; she wanted to see Mary Elizabeth. We walked to Mary Elizabeth's room and proceeded to knock on the door. Elizabeth presented a thank you gift to Mary Elizabeth. The gift? A chicken—a live chicken! Families in this community struggle to have enough to eat and only have chicken on special occasions. Chickens are costly. Because Elizabeth had received something of high value from us, she gave something of very high value to Mary Elizabeth.

I named the new chicken *Sozo*, which is the Greek word meaning "to save, heal, and deliver." The chicken had been "delivered" by someone who had been "delivered!"

There are many stories of God healing spirit, soul, and body. 1000 healings? I say yes with no exaggerations! As we go around the world, preaching, teaching, and releasing the Kingdom of heaven, there are at least fifteen to twenty different healings in every location. I mean, that is why we go. That is why we preach. When God shows up, the supernatural shows up. EVERY TIME! EVERY TIME!

THIS ELIJAH GENERATION, THESE LIONS, WILL GO OUT WITH HEALING!

---

1. Teilhard De Chardin, *The Phenomenon of Man* (*Le Phénomène Humain*), 1955, France.

5

SUCH A THING AS GLORY

Rich Mullins, in the '80s, wrote a wonderful song entitled, "Such a Thing as Glory." It is a moving song that inspires me to go after the glory of God. He waxed poetic about God's glory in a descriptive prose that only a brilliant songwriter could do. However, it left me hungrier for the glory of God, as I'm sure it was intended. Maybe the purpose of the poet was to do just that: to create more questions than answers.

Some things are just hard to answer and I think the "glory of God" is one of them. It seems to be a *conundrum* or a riddle, hidden to the human eye. Perhaps it's best explained by the words of Jesus, "Whoever has ears to hear what the Spirit is saying, let him hear." I remember hearing the word used by Alan Greenspan, Federal Reserve Chairman, several years ago. He waxed on about the economy being a conundrum as he questioned the actions of the financial powers of the world.

There are other things that are hard to understand:

- Why didn't Noah swat those two mosquitoes?
- Why do people constantly return to the refrigerator

with hopes that something new to eat has materialized?

- Why is it called rush hour when you don't move?
- Why aren't there father-in-law jokes?
- Why couldn't the professor on Gilligan's Island fix a boat if he could make a radio out of coconuts?

Solomon, the wisest man that ever lived, spoke of conundrums:

> There are three things that are too amazing for me, four that I do not understand: the way of an eagle in the sky, the way of a snake on a rock, the way of a ship in the high seas, and the way of a man with a maiden...who says, "I've done nothing wrong." (Prov. 30:18-20)

Even more pertinent, Solomon displays our quest to solve this conundrum: "It is the glory of God to conceal a matter; to search out a matter is the glory of kings" (Prov. 25:2) and we shall search it out!

The apparent puzzle: The presence of God is *glory*. If God is glory, then why are we called upon to give Him glory? See, if He is the great *I AM*—omniscient, omnipresent, omnipotent, the epitome of love, peace, joy; complete, perfect, lacking in nothing—then why does He need you and me to give Him glory? Why does He need us to give Him something that He's pretty much cornered the market on already? Again, if He is complete, needing nothing, then what does He need with us?

He is the manifest presence of glory! He is what the Old Testament refers to as *chabod*. This Hebrew word is best described as "weight, heaviness, worthiness, reputation, or honor." The temple was built as a residence for his glory presence (1 Chron. 22:5). David knew of God's glory when the Ark of the Covenant was carried to the Holy of Holies (2

Sam. 6). The glory was so powerful, it killed Uzzah when he touched it (vs. 6). Please notice that Uzzah was not a priest; he wasn't allowed to handle the glory. We are now a royal priesthood (1 Pet. 2:9) and can handle the glory! Moses recognized the power of His glory (Exod. 33). When God's presence was not enough, he wanted to see His glory. Glory changed Moses' appearance to the point that people needed sunglasses for viewing, so to speak (Exod. 34:33). The presence of the Lord always changed the atmosphere! More of His glory produced more transformation!

In the New Testament, the Greek word *doxa* expresses our transformation from glory to glory: "And we with unveiled faces all reflect the Lord's glory, are being transformed into His likeness with ever-increasing glory, which comes from the Lord, who is the Spirit" (2 Cor. 3:18). Though the context is referring to the lesser glory of the Old Testament, Paul assures us there is still more glory than what we now have. Glory is never static! God is either filling us or we are leaking Him. "Be filled with the Holy Spirit and not drunk with wine" (Eph. 5:18). The fullness of Christ is the "hope of glory," even the "certainty" of glory (Col. 1:27). "The mystery of His riches have been disclosed to the saints" (vs. 26). This glory is given to the saints through His Holy Spirit, His Presence!

Of the four hundred times the word *glory*, or its derivative, is used in the Bible (approximately 135 times in the New Testament), it is only a glimpse of the manifest presence of God. This is by no means an exhaustive study, but only a brief explanation of God's glory. It is a working definition describing man's contact with the presence of God.

"Arise, shine, for your light has come, and the glory of the Lord rises upon you...but the Lord rises upon you and

His glory appears over you" (Isa. 60:1). He wants to shine on us. The glory was taken away from man in the garden by the enemy and is now restored through Jesus Christ (Col. 1:17-21).

WHEN PAPA SHOWS UP, HE SHOWS OFF HIS CHARACTER—LOVE!

When I receive the glory of God, I am receiving a bit of heaven, the NOW of the Kingdom of God. It is the manifestation of His presence. When Papa shows up, He shows off His character—LOVE! We are being transformed (2 Cor. 3:18). We are transformed, sanctified, purified, and healed as God pours more and more of His "fullness" into us, clay vessels. Paul writes of the Christian's walk as "being filled" with His "fullness." (See Eph. 1:23; 3:19; 4:13 and 5:18 where Paul intensifies the use of the Greek noun *plaroma* and the verb *plaroo* meaning, "fullness" and "to be filled," respectively.)

When I give glory to God, it is not just an act or prayer of thanksgiving, although that is part of it. Very succinctly, it is the magnification of God's presence of Himself mirrored back to God because of His great love—through the heat and trial of life with thankfulness of praise and worship. We now reflect and mirror back what God has put in us (2 Cor. 3:18). "Worthy is the Lamb, who was slain, to receive power…and honor and glory and praise" (Rev. 5:13). "For yours is the kingdom and the power and the glory forever" (Matt. 6:13, NASB). The book of Psalms is full of phrases like "give God glory," "give Him praise and honor and glory," "declare His glory," and on and on. Our privilege in life is to live a life of praise and glory for Him! To that, there is no argument!

It seems that we are given glory to give back glory! It's almost a circle, if you will. I receive glory to give back glory. Whatever love, peace, or wealth that I have is His! I give it back. We mirror His image because we are His sons. We are no longer servants, but as sons, we give Him glory in whatever we do! We give Him glory!

THE PUZZLE IS ANSWERED: We receive glory to give it back to Him.

Spinning Wheel

I love the song by Blood Sweat and Tears, "Spinning Wheel." It begins, "What goes up must come down. Spinning wheel got to go round." Though the author may not have intentionally thought of God, it is quite prophetic: "Someone is waiting just for you; spinning wheel is spinning true. Drop all your troubles by the river side; ride a painted pony let the spinning wheel fly." The whole song could be about God, but the "spinning wheel" really depicts the glory of God. God has established His residence (glory) in us through His Holy Spirit. Jesus made sure of this on the cross and His subsequent resurrection. He had to die to give us His presence. He gives us more and we give Him glory. What goes up must come down!

The presence of God and the glory seem to be somewhat different in the Bible. Moses was in God's presence (Exod. 33:14) and then he asked to see God's glory (Exod. 33:18). Likened to that, we receive His presence now through His Holy Spirit and then, we grow and move from "glory to glory" (2 Cor. 3:18). We are being transformed by His glory (2 Cor. 3). There is no hard case to separate God's presence from His glory, however. I think we would be in error to dissect God in this manner. Though there is no qualitative separation of God expressed here, there may be a quantitative outpouring of God on human flesh. We just can't handle all of God at once. Papa showed Moses His goodness, one characteristic of Himself, in a bite-sized piece (Exod. 33:19-20). Likewise, He does the same for us today: "glory to glory." I have demonstrated the growth and manifestation of that glory at the end of this chapter. I may have become overzealous with the charts, but they show a continuum of God's glory in our lives and how we need Him in every aspect of our lives. For us to grow—or be transformed—in any characteristic, experience, or sanctification process, it all depends on Him!! (See the Appendix.)

It all depends on God; it all depends on us. The first part of this statement is easy to digest, but the second part appears to be contradictory and maybe even a bit misguided at first glance. However, this is the spinning wheel, the glory circle. He first loved us; obviously, it all depends on God. It? "It" is life and all of its realities. It all depends on us? How can this be? What would you say if I told you that He really depends on you and me to get the job done? Moreover, what would you say if I told you that it really depends on us to establish His Kingdom, power, and glory? Heresy? No!

The fall of the enemy revisited: When Satan fell, it was a horrific blow to the Kingdom of God. The devastation was great even though God knew it was coming. God had to clean house and He did: "How you have fallen from heaven, O morning star [some translations have "Lucifer" here], son of the dawn! You have been cast down to the earth...but you are brought down to the grave, to the depths of the pit" (Isa. 14:12-15).

The third angel sounded his trumpet, and a great star,

blazing like a torch, fell from the sky on a third of the rivers and on the sprigs of water—the name of the star is Wormwood [describing his demise, eaten by worms in Isa. 14:11]…a third of the sun was struck, a third of the moon, and a third of the stars [stars representing angels, Rev. 1:20], so that a third of them turned dark. A third… (Rev. 8:12)

And there was war in heaven. Michael and his angels fought against the dragon, and the dragon and his angels fought back. But he was not strong enough, and they lost their place in heaven. The great dragon was hurled down—that ancient serpent called the devil, or Satan, who leads the whole world astray. He was hurled to the earth and his angels with him. (Rev. 12:7-9)

John Milton's *Paradise Lost* allegorizes this scene with much liberty granted to the text. In the Bible, the imagery suggests that a third of all God had created was fallen to the point of no return. Satan had tried to "raise his throne above the stars of God" and "to make himself like *El Elyon* [the Most High]" (Isa. 14:13-14). Again, a third of all God created, a third of His Glory, was destroyed; Satan had taken it away. Heaven had been given a blow, but was certainly not defeated. Satan believed he could take advantage of God's love and grace, so he tried to take Him. Satan saw the continual inward spiral of God's love and grace as an innate weakness; yet Satan failed to see God's justice and power. God's authority, power, wisdom, and justice outwitted the enemy and destroyed him.

Satan is destroyed, he was destroyed, and he is being destroyed! He has fallen and he is still falling. He left the presence of God and is still leaving God's presence. As Satan leaves, he becomes more murderous, manipulative, and destructive. As he continues to leave the presence of God, the world gets darker. Satan becomes more evil and his weapons are more sinister than ever! A people grasp for security and hope in a world of darkness. However, politics and economic strategies will not save the earth; only Jesus and His glory have the power to save.

So should we say that God was down, but not out? There was great loss, but nothing of His omniscience, omnipotence, omnipresence, or His character was lost. He is still God, yet the glory, radiance, and at least a third of heaven had been lost. This is the bad news.

The GOOD NEWS is that the bad news was wrong. Satan thought he could take on God in God's own weakness—which is His love. Satan did not know that love is God's strength and power. He loves so much that He created you and me from the same earth from which Satan was hurled and now we are to re-establish His glory. He invests His glory into mankind by the blood of Jesus Christ and He creates more glory by the work of Holy Spirit. Praise God for such a plan! We are His workmanship and His Holy Spirit makes regular deposits in us. I am thankful Jesus left this earth so that His Holy Spirit could come and work through us, establishing His glory, establishing His Kingdom, establishing the realities of Heaven on earth. Jesus is taking back the land that was lost—through you and me. We are part of that continual work of glory which I call the *Glory Wheel*.

GLORY OF GOD

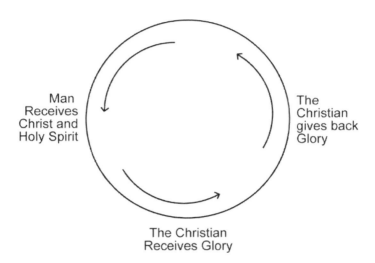

Man Receives Christ and Holy Spirit

The Christian gives back Glory

The Christian Receives Glory

God's glory, His Love, the essence of who He is, belongs to God and God alone. He, ALONE, stands complete. He doesn't need us for Him to be Him!! However, He is love and love, by its very nature, is to be given and received. Love has to be reciprocated to fulfill itself. God has chosen to show His glory to us: "His intent was that now, through the church, the manifold wisdom of God should be made known to the rulers and authorities in the heavenly realms" (Eph. 3:10).

LOVE HAS TO BE RECIPROCATED TO FULFILL ITSELF.

In His infinite wisdom, God chose us to participate with Heaven. HE CHOSE US to re-establish His glory. It works like a savings and loan. He loans us His glory. We save it, not by laying up treasures, but by depositing it in others and it just grows and grows. We then give Him glory by thanking Him and giving Him praise!! Pretty easy, isn't it? The beauty of it all is the master plan of the glory of God. The more we give God the glory, the more we, in turn, receive His glory. And the cycle continues. He gives, you give, and He gives more—with interest. Therefore, the more we have, the more we have to give, and He gives even more, and so on it goes!

Biblical Circles

Paul prays "…that out of His glorious riches He may strengthen you with power through His Spirit in your inner being" (Eph. 3:16). Now watch this circle around.

Now to him who is able to do immeasurably more than all we ask or imagine, according to His power that is at work within us, to him be glory in the church and in Christ Jesus… for ever and ever.
(Eph. 3:20)

See the circle: we receive the glory so that Christ may receive the glory.

Throughout John 17, Jesus speaks of the glory that He is about to receive and the glory He is giving to the Father and to the Church. Follow the circle: "Glorify your Son, that your Son may glorify you" (John 17:1). That's pretty obvious; now look at this: "I have brought you glory on earth by completing the work you have given me to do. And now, Father, glorify me in your presence with the glory I had with you before the world began" (John 17:4-5). The circle seems continue in these two verses: "…and glory has come to me through them [the disciples]" (17:10); "I have given them the glory that you gave me" (17:22). Wow, this is good! I have to give Papa all praise, glory, and honor that is due Him! He is so good.

Scripture is inundated with this circle of giving and receiving. The very nature of God is to love: giving and receiving. The main principle of the Kingdom of God is giving bountifully and receiving bountifully. The cycle of God's glory is continual and ever increasing.

God has chosen this Elijah Generation to spread the gospel in ways like never before. As the enemy intensifies the darkness, the Heavenly Father is pouring out His Spirit on His sons and daughters. We get to participate in the things of God as if heaven depends on it. We are establishing, totally dependent on God, the Kingdom of God. We are restoring that which the enemy has stolen—at least one third of heaven. The enemy has not only stolen from us personally, but from our Father. God is just and His anger and judgments toward those who come against us are written in the Old and New Testaments. "Vengeance is mine," says the Lord (Rom. 12:19).

The Glory Wheel

Ruth Heflin, an old saint, passionate to behold the glory of God, used to say, "Praise...until the spirit of worship comes. Worship...until the glory comes. Then...stand in the glory!"[1] God gives you as much you can handle. If you are accustomed to twenty minutes on Sunday morning, that's about all you can handle. However, as you praise Him, He is so faithful to come. Bit by bit, our whole being (spirit, soul, and body) becomes one with Him. It doesn't happen all at once. God knows what will happen if there is too much of His glory in our flesh. So, little by little, great gain comes in being with Him. The more you stand in the glory, the more you are transformed. With that transformation, you become a competent minister of the gospel. Praise and worship bring in the glory. The more you stand in the glory, the more God will stand in you. To the degree you give glory to God is the degree that God will allow you to carry His glory.

THE MORE YOU STAND IN THE GLORY, THE MORE YOU ARE TRANSFORMED.

Don't be like the nine lepers who were healed and failed to say thank you. Jesus gave us a key to His Kingdom in Luke 17:11-17. Praise and giving glory to God are the pathway for the River to flow.

Jonah, in a belly of a whale, cried out in distress for seven verses of Jonah 2. Then in 2:9, he made the sacrifice of praise and was spit out on dry land. The key here is to praise God when you are in the belly of a whale. David found this to be true in Psalms. Hezekiah's prayer of repentance and praise gave him fifteen more years of life. The praise and shouts of the people of God at Jericho brought the walls down.

GIVE GOD PRAISE AND THANKSGIVING
AND THE GLORY COMES!
GIVE GOD PRAISE AND THANKSGIVING
AND THE GLORY COMES!

Praise breaks the heavy yoke. The glory comes and transforms. We receive more capacity for His glory. We get to do more of the miracles, signs and wonders. We give Him glory............and the circle continues.

Why?

Why do I need more of His glory? Because life is no

longer worth living without Him! Life can be quite boring and the endless pursuit of stuff to fill us up actually doesn't fill us, but leads to death! We choose Him! We choose Life!

His glory brings the deep things of God. 1 Cor. 2

His glory brings peace.

His glory brings the oil of healing and miracles.

His glory transforms. 2 Cor. 3 and 4

His glory brings revelation. 2 Cor. 4:6

His glory brings whatever is needed at the time.

His glory is prosperity, purpose, power, grace, and love.

Glory Wheel: Give glory to God and see what He does!

WHAT GOES UP, MUST COME DOWN.
GLORY WHEEL, GOT TO GO ROUND!

Transformation

His glory is transformational. "And we, who with unveiled faces all reflect the Lord's glory, are being transformed into His likeness with ever-increasing glory, which comes from the Lord, who is the Spirit" (1 Cor. 3:18). The following chart is a fair representation of the display found in Bob Sorge's book, *Glory: When Heaven Invades Earth*. He goes into detail on pages 56 and 57 about the degrees of God's glory. Succinctly put, Sorge says, "The following diagram is my crude and inadequate attempt to try to illustrate the gradient intensities of God's personhood. Take it for what it's worth because this diagram only begins to portray the awesomeness of God's Presence and Glory." I agree totally.

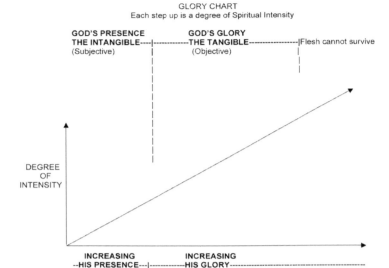

See Bob Sorge's website: www.oasishouse.net (Used by permission).

The Lord allowed me to flesh this out a bit. Are there some signs along the way to help us know if we are growing in the glory? One might ask, "Am I increasing in His glory and how will I know when I get there?" Hopefully, the following chart may bring Scriptural clarity to a seemingly intangible process. Keeping it real, this chart is also an arbitrary graph put in practical terms, bringing more clarity to our generally ethereal and abstract descriptions of God's glory. Hopefully, this measuring device may spur us on to grow in His grace and power. (See the Appendix also.) Growing in the glory of God is the essence of real life.

RISING DEGREE OF GLORY
Bible examples, representing the rising intensity of His glory

Key: This chart represents an increase in spiritual intensity as one rises in God's glory

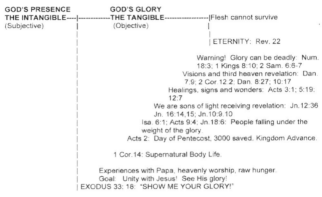

GOD'S PRESENCE   GOD'S GLORY
THE INTANGIBLE----|------------THE TANGIBLE----------------|Flesh cannot survive
(Subjective) | (Objective) |

| ETERNITY: Rev. 22

Warning! Glory can be deadly: Num. 18:3; 1 Kings 8:10; 2 Sam. 6:6-7
Visions and third heaven revelation: Dan. 7:9; 2 Cor. 12:2; Dan. 8:27; 10:17
Healings, signs and wonders: Acts 3:1; 5:19; 12:7
We are sons of light receiving revelation: Jn. 12:36 Jn. 16:14,15; Jn.10:9,10
Isa. 6:1; Acts 9:4; Jn.18:6: People falling under the weight of the glory.
Acts 2: Day of Pentecost, 3000 saved, Kingdom Advance.

1 Cor.14: Supernatural Body Life.

Experiences with Papa, heavenly worship, raw hunger.
Goal: Unity with Jesus! See His glory!
| EXODUS 33: 18: "SHOW ME YOUR GLORY!"

Exodus 33:14,15: "If your Presence does not go with us..."

Great music, good fellowship, passion for Jesus.
Goal: Unity with the Believers.
In pain there is solace: "I will never leave you nor forsake you" (Heb.13:5).

Matt. 28:20: "...and lo, I am with you always."

Acts 2:38: Repent and be baptized and receive.

Born again John 3:3,16.

GOD'S PRESENCE-|-----------GOD'S GLORY-------------------|----------------------

1. Ruth Heflin, *Glory: Experiencing the Atmosphere of Heaven* (Hagerstown, PA: The McDougal Publishing Company, 1990), p. viii.
2. Bob Sorge, *Glory: When Heaven Invades Earth* (Greenwood, MO: Oasis House, 2000), p. 56-57.

6

THE FATHER'S HEART: SONSHIP

"In bringing many sons to glory…Jesus is not ashamed to call them brothers." The entire second chapter of Hebrews secures identity for us, with verses ten and eleven specifically expressing the desire of Papa's heart.

> …you will live because those who are led by the Spirit of God are sons of God. For you did not receive a spirit that makes you a slave again to fear, but you received the Spirit of sonship. And by Him we cry, "Abba, Father." The Spirit Himself testifies with our spirit that we are God's children. Now if we are children, then we are heirs—heirs of God and co-heirs with Christ, if indeed we share in his sufferings in order that we may also share in His glory. (Rom. 8:14-17)

"How great is the love the Father has lavished on us, that we should be called children of God! AND THAT IS WHAT WE ARE!" (1 John 3:1)

We can preach and teach all about the different nuances of identity, but until God reveals His sonship to each of us individually, we will occupy our station in life on the other side of the cross. We will embrace the suffering and constant debasing of the flesh and never really KNOW Him and the power of His resurrection. I pray that the eyes of our hearts would be open to know the hope to which He has called us, to see the glorious inheritance that we have and His incomparably great power, the same power that raised Jesus from the dead. I also pray that His Spirit of wisdom and revelation would come so we would know Him better (see Eph. 1:17-20).

The world is crying out for answers because the darkness has gotten darker. Papa is about to reveal his sons in fire and glory as an Elijah Generation. He is calling us to come to Him and KNOW Him rather than just knowing about Him. God is about to shift His people from a mind-focused religion to a heart-focused relationship. From legalism to a legacy filled with awesome exploits with Him. From illegitimacy to being too legit to quit. From the tree of the knowledge of good and evil to the tree of life. From self-purpose to a son's purpose. From self-image to Christ's image. From narcissism to knowledge of Him. From pseudo-humility to boasting in Christ. From an inheritance from our parents to His inheritance. From religion to relationship. From a step-child to sonship, following His steps. From the wounds that make us run for the medications this world has to offer, to the womb of the throne room, birthing freedom. From bondage to freedom! SHIFT! NOW! In Jesus' Name! "For the creation waits in eager expectation for the sons of God to be revealed" (Rom. 8:19).

Scars

Harry Chapin's "Cat's in the Cradle" has been used to

epitomize the decay of the family in America by many Christian authors. The words are especially true for the Baby Boomer dad who was busy working to provide and fulfill the "American Dream." This song depicts the forlorn promise for intimacy. In this song, the dad will soon come home and that's when they will get together. Of course, it never happens. The child thus repeats the cycle because of his innate desire to be just like his dad. So, the lack of intimacy from the ghost of a dad is duplicated for future generations.

The next generation, known as the X Generation, cried out even more as both mom and dad were imprinted with the same role model of pursuit of the American Dream, regardless of the cost. Now as I work with the Y Generation, I am finding that the teens of today are often trying to raise their parents. The parents have become the children and vice versa. Many of today's teens are enmeshed with their parents regarding drugs, alcohol, adultery, and more. The children are living with parents who are wayward and scarred by the sins of their own parents. Wow! What do you do? All of creation is yearning for the sons and daughters to be revealed to do what? "…that the creation itself will be liberated from its bondage to decay and brought into the glorious freedom of the children of God" (Rom. 8:21). We now groan with creation as "…we wait eagerly for our adoption as sons, the redemption of our bodies" (Rom. 8:23). This is not just for later, but for NOW! The Kingdom of God is NOW! God will liberate us from the sins of the past to bring freedom to all. He heals and transforms by His glory and then shifts us into the realities of His purposes and revelation. He desires sonship and intimacy in order to breathe destiny in every one of us.

Scars result into Stars!

Papa, in His infinite love and healing, will transform our scars into *shining stars* (Phil. 2:15). With the revelation of sonship, Papa God will heal completely. So, "Dear Lord, hear my heart's cry: 'Pour it on!' Sonship—we desperately need it. Let us hear Your call and move us under Your anointing and favor, now!'"

HE DESIRES SONSHIP AND INTIMACY IN ORDER TO BREATHE DESTINY IN EVERY ONE OF US.

To Know You is to Love You

"To know, know, know you is to love, love, love you" was a 1969 hit single by Bobby Vinton. I grew up hearing that song, but had little understanding of its meaning. I knew love, but not love like Papa wanted to download! I didn't truly know Papa for years; I knew something was missing. I knew Him somewhat, but not how I wanted—my soul yearned for more. I had zeal and passion for the first twenty years of ministry, but it was actually a mixture of self-love, coupled with the need for validation. After the passion of first love was depleted by the rigors of ministry, I knew there had to be more. I recall years of anguish as I asked God, "What is love? What does it mean to *love*?" Many in my denomination purported the idea that *love* is controlled by the will and as such, it is a choice. That cold conceptual mindset left me empty, harsh, and sick! There had to be more. I cried out for more, even while my ministry was growing and I was baptizing and preaching in the name of Jesus.

Who is Jesus? How did I get to know Him? I really

thought I knew Him, but in reality, I knew *about* Him. I had a great fundamental doctrine of Jesus, but didn't have a clue about His true nature; it rocked my soul at times. Jesus was "just alright with me" (Doobie Brothers), but I acted out my lack of identity by wanting more things in this world. Thereby, given my place in the world, I desired a bigger church and confused my passion for Jesus with validation. Ministry became my identity, not Jesus. I really didn't know Jesus—I did know that! By 1988, I decided to get into the Word more and pray more. This was the beginning of my demise, the Dwight I once knew. Jesus was about to answer the cry of my heart. I was in process for a divine exchange from glory to glory. I was about to realize that to know Him is to experience His love! He had to be present. My walls were about to come down so He could enter. I allowed Him to come.

As my walls began tumbling down, I realized that there were even differences in the Greek New Testament describing this knowledge. W.E. Vine's *Expository Dictionary* points out the following:

> **ginosko** signifies "to be taking in knowledge, to come to know, recognize, understand" or "to understand completely," e.g., Mark 13:28, 29; John 13:12; John 15:18; John 21:17; 2 Cor 8:9; Heb. 10:34; 1 John 2:5; 1 John 4:2, 6 (twice); 1 John 2:4, 13; 1 John 5:2, 20. In the New Testament, *ginosko* frequently indicates a relation between the person "knowing" and the object known; in this respect, what is "known" is of value or importance to the one who knows, and, hence, the establishment of the relationship, e.g., especially of God's "knowledge," 1 Cor 8:3, "if any man love God, the same is known of

Him;" Gal. 4:9, "to be known of God;" here the "knowing" suggests approval and bears the meaning "to be approved;" 1 John 2:3, 13, 14; 1 John 4:6, 8, 16; 1 John 5:20; such "knowledge" is obtained, not by mere intellectual activity, but by operation of the Holy Spirit consequent upon acceptance of Christ.[1]

My knowledge of Him was about to change to *knowing Him*. Another Greek word in the New Testament is *oida*, usually used to convey a perception, or to see, or to have knowledge of the mind. My *oida* was vastly becoming my *ginosko*. By 1994, I was worshiping God with much of my heart and by the year 2000, the wheels on the wagon actually flew off. The Lord totally rearranged my knowing Him. I was trying to handle the Glory of the Lord my way and I needed to come to Him completely. Just as David thought he knew what was best in handling the Glory, I, too, thought my way was best. As the wheels of the wagon, or the oxen stumbled, and the Ark of the Covenant nearly fell off David's cart, I, like Uzzah, was too quick to try to catch it under my own volition. (Read 2 Sam. 6 to catch the entire metaphor.) As I experienced inner healing and a truer relationship with Jesus, I began to know Him better. He showed me that He is the answer to all my problems. I didn't know that for years. Oh, yes, as a preacher, I mimicked the cliché, but I didn't truly know. Years went by and, finally, He called me out of the desert. I was finally ready. My experience was similar to that of Moses. The first third of his life, he thought he was somebody; the next 40 years in the desert, he realized he was a nobody; the last part of his life, he realized that God could use a nobody, standing only in His Presence.

God wants to pour Himself, His very Presence, into His beloved Sons. He who has an ear to hear what the Spirit is saying, come! Come! Buy silver and gold from Me, says the Lord. We agree, the Bride and the Spirit say, Come! Come! Let the sons and daughters come! Blessed are those who eat from the tree of life; they will walk through the gates of the City!

We will never experience Him fully, nor come into our sonship until all the lies are removed. There are lies and wounds that created wrong perceptions within us and keep us in bondage which prevent the King of Glory from coming in. We say we want Him, but then quickly dismiss Him because of our unbeliefs, misbeliefs, and half-truths. The Lord wants to sanctify the whole person. Fear and love cannot co-exist. "Without faith, it is impossible to please God" (Heb. 11:6). Sonship comes by our free will saying "Yes!" We want all of Him to consume all of us.

Doctrine is no replacement for sonship. Knowing about God is like experiencing a marriage from a distance. You go to a school to learn about marriage and people, but never get the opportunity to experience relationship? About a year before I married Candy, she moved to Nashville for the summer. I was living in Atlanta and I knew the pain was going to be excruciating! The few times I drove from Atlanta to Nashville to see her, there were no speed limits that could keep my heavy foot off the gas pedal. I was like Jehu in the Bible who "drove his chariot swiftly," to say the least. I needed to see Candy because all the phone calls, all the letters, all the cards, could never compare to experiencing her presence. Her look, her being, her presence, her atmosphere, her smells, her beauty, her voice, her non-verbal communication, was tantamount to a letter or a note. I had to experience her—be in her presence. To know Candy was to love her and experience life with her. God is like this and even more so. He is supernatural and can be experienced on so many levels. Come Lord!

Whenever doctrine is **amassed** in the mind, it creates **a mess**. When a teaching is only for the mind's purpose, instead of the Spirit's, it is the knowledge that "puffs up." In other words, when you have a teaching from the Word and there is no allowance for the Holy Spirit to work, then you have legalism. The tendency and bent is for legalism. Bill Johnson states, "Any revelation from God's Word that does not lead us to an encounter with God only serves to make us more religious. The Church cannot afford 'form without power,' for it creates Christians without purpose."[2] Today we have many Christians who are without purpose. There are many young adults who are crying out for destiny in all the wrong places. Today, if you hear His Voice, listen and you will hear Him calling you to sonship. He invites you to become a part of this Elijah Generation, a generation that knows Papa's heart!

WHENEVER DOCTRINE IS AMASSED IN THE MIND, IT CREATES A MESS.

The book of Galatians addresses the subjects of religion and legalism. From the apostle Paul's writings:

A Legalist:

- Full of judgments: 2:6
- Hypocrite: 2:13
- Proud: 2:15, the knowledge that puffs up. (1 Cor. 8:1)
- No justice, for they feel they are not justified: 2:16
- Antichrist: 2:20,21. Its goal—to have religion with

"anointing."

- Having a form of godliness without power.
- Under the power of witchcraft: 3:1
- A fool and does foolish things: 3:3
- Under a yoke of slavery: 5:1
- If justified by the law, fallen away from grace: 5:4 (Guilt, condemnation, performance)
- Agitators: 5:12
- Living under the law instead of the Spirit: 5:16,17 (Full of sin)
- Legalism has no value over restraining sin (Col. 2:20-22). In fact, it does the opposite: causes you to lust.

So, understand that the law brings us to Christ to become sons of God (3:23, 26; 4:6ff). The whole purpose of the law is to bring us to the saving knowledge of Jesus Christ. Religion is no place to park, but is there to point us to Jesus. The law was to be the schoolmaster and tutor to bring us to Jesus.

No wonder there is a lack of purpose and destiny in many of our twenty-somethings. They have been led to Jesus, but that's it! The privilege of sonship is relationship, walking with Him everyday. Most churches intentionally feed crumbs because of time restraints. We are too busy to get under the fountain and splash in the River of His Presence with Him. Sonship, like any relationship, takes time! Any religion that feeds only the mind and does not allow the Holy Spirit to direct us to sonship is about to be changed. Having a form of godliness but denying His power is anathema!

Sonship is relationship. Intimacy! When I finally saw my girlfriend in Nashville (now my wife of 35 years), I was taken aback by her beauty. I just wanted to be in her presence. I would do anything to be in her presence. That's the way it is with Jesus. I just want to be in His Presence. Let us be your children, oh Lord! We declare your sonship over us!

Make these declarations right now! Say them out loud.

DECLARATIONS OF SONSHIP

➤ I have received the full rights of sonship. I have received the Spirit of His Son into my heart, who calls out "Abba, Father." I am no longer a servant nor slave, but an heir, a son. (Gal. 4: 6-8)

➤ The Father is always with me and everything He has is mine. (Luke 15:31)

➤ Christ became poor so that I might become rich in every way. (2 Cor. 8:9)

➤ I have everything that I need because the Father is able to make grace abound toward me in all things. I even have abundance for every good work. (2 Cor. 9:8)

➤ God blesses me and makes me a blessing to everyone I meet. (Gen. 12:2-3)

➤ Through faith in Christ Jesus, I am a son of God. (Gal. 3:26-29)

➤ He has made me a little lower than Himself. (Ps. 8:4-6)

➤ Since He has redeemed me to be a son, even a son of God, to rule and reign with Him, I have purpose and destiny in all things, every day. (John 10:34)

➤ I am received unconditionally, just as I am. I have been given a robe of righteousness, life, and inheritance. I have been given a ring of authority and dominion. I have been given sandals of honor to eat the Bread of Life around the "banquet eating table."

➤ Since He has clothed me in righteousness, it is not my

conduct that determines my sonship, but my sonship determines my conduct.

➢ Since I am a son, He sees my robe of righteousness bought and paid for by Jesus. He does not see my failures and sin.

➢ I will abide in the house of the Lord forever, for I am His son. I know Him, not about Him. I know the Father's heart. I react to the things He reacts to and love the things He loves. He longs to reveal the deep things of His heart to me. I long to know the extravagance of His love and the generosity of His lavished love.

➢ Your love is stronger than death, many waters cannot quench Your love. I am your son/daughter. You are my Daddy. I am your son/daughter. You are my Daddy. You will never forsake me nor leave me. I am precious in your sight. You have an unreal inheritance for me that I can begin to access now, because all you have is mine.

Thank you, Daddy. Thank you.

From Religion to Relationship
From Orphans to Sons

Recently, I was "soaking" or hanging out with Jesus and I heard Him say, "I'M CALLING YOU!...my son." Wow, how cool, I thought. Yes, I have a calling on my life and God is revealing my destiny and what I am to do. I thought, great, now I'll know what to do next. Then I heard it another way, "I'm calling you: 'MY SON!' " Suddenly, I understood it in a completely different way. The first understanding is doing; the second, is being. Now that was revelation! The revelation of sonship is desperately desired! It changes everything.

HE MOVES US:

From lambs to lions.

From religion to relationship.

From rebellion to relationship.

From orphans to sons.

From servants to friendship.

From relying on our own righteousness to accepting His.

From performance to acts of faith.

From selfish motivations to honoring the King.

From knowing about Him to knowing Him.

From paranoia to transparency.

From fear of authority to having authority.

From living in the flesh to living in the Spirit.

From control to faith in Papa.

From festering wounds to freedom and healing.

From sacrificing a few moments of earthly pleasure for eternal heavenly treasure.

From playboy to playful son.

From pornography to purity.

From idolatry to intimacy.

From barnyard chickens to soaring eagles.

From pittance to abundance.

From sadness to joy.

From entrapments to wisdom and a mature conscience.

From my pleasure to the Father's pleasure.

From negative habits to His positive Presence.

From living for the moment to living with His eyes and vision.

From the triggers of life to living in Perfect Peace, whose mind is stayed on Him.

From hunger to being filled.

From lust to love.

From anger to resolution, peace, healing, and fulfillment.

From self-image to Christ's image.

From wandering in arid places to identity and value.

From self-exaltation to Christ's exaltation.

From craving a platform for ministry to saying, "I just don't need it anymore."

From the plan of the enemy to Papa's plan.

From guilt and shame to redemption.

From anger and distrust towards God, to restoration by Papa's love.

From independence to an inseparable bond with Papa.

From being captivated by our gifts and talents to being captivated by His look.

From lack of gifts and talents to relying on His strength and love.

From shallowness to a depth of riches that has no end.

From the Kingdom of heaven that is "not yet" to the Kingdom, NOW!

I've told my story in a lot of different ways. Yet the path hasn't been filled with great leaps of growth and powerful exploits alone. Like Elijah under the tree after the great victory against the prophets of Baal, I have had my own "dark nights of the soul." I've looked at my dry periods of life and have asked the question over and over, "Why?" I evaluate those times by asking, "What could I have done differently?" I realize that God healed me and changed me drastically. I probably needed to go through "process" in order to build my faith in Jesus. I know all the right answers, but I look for a common thread in the down times of my life, where even sin ruled! If I can be so simplistic, let me say this: WHEN I PULLED AWAY FROM PAPA, I FAILED MISERABLY. WHEN I WAS CLOSE TO HIM, HE WAS MY ROCK

AND STRONGHOLD! When I was intimate and close to Him, He was close to me; but when I chose to put other things and idols first, then He left. Whether by devotions, Bible reading, quiet times, soaking, worshiping, or whatever you want to call it, being with Him is crucial.

INTIMACY, IRONICALLY, SATISFIES OUR IMMEDIATE HUNGER WHILE ALL THE WHILE CREATING A LONGING FOR MORE OF HIM.

Intimacy is the goal for everything we are and we do. He has created us to be in fellowship with Him. From the time of Adam, He has wanted us to be with Him in the Garden; now He desires a restored relationship with His son, daughter, and bride. Intimacy is the goal of inner transformation and healing, not the side effect. He expands our identity and value as we sit at His feet like Mary. Intimacy enlarges our capacity to hold more of Him. Intimacy, ironically, satisfies our immediate hunger while all the while creating a longing for more of Him. Let God change the orphan poverty spirit within you. The removal of the orphan spirit can't be cast out; moreover, it is the total transformation of spirit, soul, and body. It comes by being with Him, soaking and marinating in His Presence.

How do you SOAK?
Let go:
"Come to me all who are weary and burdened and I will give you rest." (Matt.11:28)
"Work hard to enter the rest." (Heb. 4:9-11)

"He leads me beside quiet waters; He restores my soul." (Ps. 23:1-3)

"(You) search your heart and be silent." (Ps. 4:4)

Now is the time for you to let go and enter His rest. You may want to read the Bible, but I strongly encourage you to turn on some worship music, not praise music that arouses your flesh, but soft worship music that arouses your spirit. Now find a comfortable place to position yourself to receive what Papa wants to tell you. Allow the busyness of your thoughts to quiet. If you think of things that you need to do, then write them down and be done with them. This is a time for you to enter His gates. Surrender your spirit, body, and soul to the Lord. Tell your soul to be quiet and tell your spirit to rise up and be one with God. Focus on the Lord's Presence and rest in faith! Do it again and again until you, a lamb, become a lion.

Lean in:

"Who is this coming up from the wilderness, **leaning** on her beloved?" (Song of Sol. 8:5)

"One of them, the disciple whom Jesus loved, was **reclining next** to **Him... leaning** back against Jesus..." (John 13: 22-25)

"...let the beloved of the Lord rest secure in Him, for He shields him all day long, and the one the Lord loves **rests between his shoulders.**" (Deut. 33:12)

"Mary, sitting at Jesus' feet, chose the better thing." (Luke 10:39)

"Be still and know that 'I am' God." (Ps. 46:10)

"Taste and see that the Lord is good." (Ps. 34:8)

"You, God, are my God, earnestly I seek you." (Ps. 63:1)

Enter into His rest. He may want to touch you in

different ways in order to meet with you face to face. You want to have a real encounter with God. This may be the day, or maybe God needs to clean you up a bit first. Perhaps He needs to clear out the garbage brought in by the enemy. Wounds need to be healed. That lie the enemy branded upon your spirit that reverberates throughout your soul, "You can't trust Jesus anymore," needs to be softened a bit before the weed is uprooted. The condition of the heart needs marinating by the Presence of the Lord before all the weeds are torn out. We can only stand so much! Papa, in His infinite love and wisdom, knows when and how to do it.

Listen:
"…the sheep listen to His voice." "…they know His voice." "…my sheep know me." "…They too will listen to my voice." (John 10:3, 4, 14, 16)
"Rest in the Lord and wait patiently." (Ps. 37:7)
"My heart says of You, 'Seek His Face!' Your face, Lord, I will seek." (Ps. 27:8)
"You make known to me the path of life; you will fill me with joy in Your presence, with eternal pleasures at Your right hand." (Ps. 16:11)

INTIMACY WITH GOD IS THE KEY TO FRUITFULNESS IN EVERY AREA OF LIFE.

So, you need to be quiet and listen. Prayer is a two-way communication and now's the time to listen. He will show you unsearchable truths. God may touch you in different ways. He may touch your emotions, your body, or your spirit. You may laugh, cry, or even shake. You may have a vision, or He may take you to a memory. He may bring healing or a deep rest. You may even go to sleep. He will give you what you need that day, that hour, that moment.

Abide with Him. Intimacy with God is the key to fruitfulness in every area of life. His presence in us will draw other people to Him. As we become more infected by His presence, others around us will be affected. We will become a people who change cultures. As we spend time in the secret place, we begin to walk in the Spirit rather than out of personal striving. We become dependent with the ease of His Anointing rather than the coerciveness of our independence. Bad habits will cease. Fruit will abound!

Sons and Daughters will be born again, again. A baptism of love will fall. Revelation will flow. Lambs will become lions.

Is it Real and Can I do it?

I met Jack some time ago. He had been a Christian for several years, yet he was in position for the Lord to set him on fire. He came to one of our "Hearing God" classes. I kept my eye on Jack; he seemed somewhat aloof and I wasn't sure what to make of him. I really wondered about him when he asked to record our sessions. I didn't know if I was ready for that—and why did he want to record us? Time would tell, and it did. After a series of meetings, classes, and prayer sessions, I got to know Jack. Through our internship ministry school and a mission trip together, I witnessed a transformation begin in Jack as he began to know and experience Papa God and find his own true identity in sonship. His identity has been changed by the glory of the Father and his destiny is secured in the knowledge of that glory. Jack will say that "doing the things of God" is real and I can attest to the fact that he readily gets words of knowledge and prophecy;

healing moves through him constantly. Praise God!

Jill came to us full of grace and joy. She was beautiful in many ways. My wife and I had a prayer session or two with her and found her to be so innocent. I enjoyed having her in our classes and on the mission field as well. She was a real saint in the Lord and heard God readily. As she dealt with the inner trappings that held her captive, she became more free and confident to move in His ways. Jill has come into her true identity with more prayer, more of the Presence of God in her life, and hanging around the anointing. She completed an internship with Iris Ministries in Mozambique and knows there's much more ahead in this life with our big God. Jill is a powerful commodity in the trade winds of the Holy Spirit. She now knows who she is and is a formidable force against the wiles of the enemy.

Jack and Jill went up the hill to fetch a pail of water. They both live on that hill of the Lord. They went up the hill on different sides and found Jesus and His power. Together they are asking what's next?! Every step they take is their destiny for they both know Papa is in charge. Their heart's cry is intimacy with Him and a release of His Kingdom power through their lives.

---

1. W.E. Vine, An Expository Dictionary of New Testament Words (New Jersey, Fleming H. Revell Company, 1940).

2. Bill Johnson, *When Heaven Invades Earth* (Shippensburg, PA: Destiny Image, 2003), p. 87.

7

THE FATHER'S HEART: HEAR HIS VOICE

Megabytes, gigabytes, or even terabytes of information and life-changing experiences have been downloaded to my wife and me over the last few years. We have eagerly shared with open hearts the understanding God has given us. Papa wants this Elijah Generation to hear His voice because it is crucial in receiving the Kingdom initiatives that He desires to release. There is a terabyte for you, for everyone!

Years before Candy and I had any understanding that God could, and would, speak to us all the time, the prophetic gifting inside us would manifest itself incognito. Many years ago, we were semi-relegated to believe that God would only speak to us concerning big things like marriage, ministry, and the like. Little did we know that God is always speaking. Once, while patronizing a local restaurant, I began looking around the room. I noticed a woman with a child with her and I recall saying to Candy, "That woman was just divorced and she is without a job, wondering how to pay the bills." I didn't know what to do with that at the time; my wife just shrugged it off with a "yeah, right." She did this because I found myself repeating this exercise whenever we went out.

After awhile, when my scattered gift of discernment got the best of me, I would feel and hear people's distress, so I began giving away money. Usually, I would just offer to pay for a meal or give away $20. In those beginning stages of hearing God, He was speaking constantly and we were about to awaken to the sound of His voice.

As discussed previously, I really began to seek God in the late eighties. At times I would hear God speak directly, at other times, indirectly. I learned to even hear Him in the clamor and noise of my mind. I had a huge decision to make around 1985 regarding the Masonic Lodge. I "was raised," or joined the masons, but after hearing God and wrestling with the issue, I finally decided it was wrong. I had to renounce all the oaths I had made. It was stressful getting there, but after my resignation, a huge burden was lifted. Later, I was delivered from that spirit. God confirmed my right decision by a sign. I received a newsletter from the "grand master poopan" saying that we serve a god of many names; it may be God, Buddah, Zoaster, or whomever. I knew I didn't want any part of that.

I continued my pursuit of hearing God like a child with a new toy. I began praying and fasting for an answer from God for direction on a new vision for the church I was pastoring. I felt like God had given me an answer for the church—to acquire land, build a baseball field, and build a new auditorium. In my neophyte excitement, I approached the elders with this vision. Well, shall we say we all had a big chuckle over that idea. In my youthful zeal, I didn't really know how to present the revelation and understanding I had.

God soon called me to another church where we experienced tremendous growth and success. As mentioned before, 1994 was a time of shift and change. While God was healing people, the leadership had a different idea as to how that should look. God told me one thing that changed my life, "If you stop talking about the healings, then I will stop healing!" That one statement changed our course in life. My life, all of my family, and many who God touched through me, would never be the same. Leaving the denomination I served for many years was actually best for all. By the end of the year, hearing God's voice had become a natural part of our lives. We attended several conferences that year which allowed me to hear and receive prophetic words as well as give them. I was having the time of my life. I felt like I had died and gone to heaven.

BY THE END OF THE YEAR, HEARING GOD'S VOICE HAD BECOME A NATURAL PART OF OUR LIVES.

Moving Heaven and Earth

In 1995, we traveled to Anaheim, California, with several other Vineyard pastors (I had planted a Vineyard church by then) for the annual pastors' conference with John Wimber. It was great! Even the trip back had some grandiose moments. On the flight back, our trip was routed from Anaheim to Minneapolis and then to Atlanta. That's a long route to Atlanta. (May I note that the strangest flight I've ever taken was from the Dominican Republic to New York to Washington to Atlanta. There seems to be a quicker way!) Anyway, during our Minneapolis stop, it was uncomfortably hot in the terminal. It was so hot, even all the ice had melted! There was no air conditioning in the terminal. They were having a heat wave with a temperature of 95 degrees. As we boarded the plane, I noticed that the scorching heat was being followed by some huge, dark thunderclouds. As I went by an attendant, I mentioned something about the dark clouds. She responded with a quip that the clouds would probably ground us on the tarmac. I don't know, maybe she heard from God (or the weather report); however, she was right. As we began to taxi from one side of the airport to the other, the pilot announced over the PA system that a huge cloud was coming toward us and we would have to return to the south side. When we got to the south side, we waited and waited for another thirty minutes. The pilot announced again that we had to wait for the cloud to break up and then the control tower would give us the go ahead.

At that time, something came over me. I knew I needed to pray out loud and speak declarations for clear skies. I asked Joel, who was traveling with our group, if we could pray together. He said to meet him at his seat in a few minutes. I knew Joel didn't understand—how could he? I felt pushed by the Lord to do this "thing." I was beginning to feel that feeling you have when you know you should have done something and you didn't! I didn't want to feel that way! I knew what I needed to do. I also knew if I didn't obey, I would miss this God opportunity and regret it later. So, as I was about to stand up, the pilot once again came over the intercom and shared his regrets about not taking off and that we were still waiting for the clouds to break up. With a voice of frustration, he said we might have to taxi to the runway on the other side again. I then stood up and announced: I KNOW ALL OF YOU ARE AS TIRED OF WAITING ON THIS PLANE AS I AM, SO WILL YOU PRAY WITH ME? I asked the Lord to move the clouds and give us the breakthrough. I took authority over the enemy and told him to leave. I said a few other things and sat down. Then, suddenly within sixty seconds, the pilot said, "It's kinda strange, but the clouds just broke open and the control tower has given us clearance for take off. Buckle your seat belts, please. Attendants, get the cabin ready for take-off." HOME RUN! Everyone in the plane begin to yell and clap. People came by, patting me on my back. One guy said, "How'd you do that?" Oh, God did it, not me! Another, "How much does that cost?" I quickly remarked, "Your whole life." Needless to say, I had to give the glory to God and not take it on myself. I did get to share about Jesus with several people and one couple actually followed me into the Atlanta terminal, asking for more! I told them that Jesus really hears us and we can hear His voice. Johnny (Atlanta Vineyard Pastor at that time) was standing nearby, so I invited them to the Atlanta Vineyard. I'm not sure if they made it, but Papa wanted to show His power to many there. He did a lot that day!

I must say that I've had several airplane experiences like that. I have prayed and prophesied for many attendants and passengers at random times. On one occasion, God called on me to pray and jumpstart a plane and I failed. I missed it. The plane was waiting at the gate and wasn't taking off due to air traffic reasons. I was supposed to stand up and declare. I didn't. I was afraid. I repented for not obeying and told the Lord if that ever happened again, I would be his man. Six months later, I was called upon for the task. Papa was able to restore me in that area by allowing a stalled plane to get moving out of Sierra Leone after I prayed. Please notice that I had prophesied to hundreds within those six months, but I needed for Papa to restore me in His own way. Praise God.

There are many more stories. Candy and I have

prophesied many words of God, bringing hope, life, encouragement, strength and comfort to others. We love seeing Papa release words to people, bringing a sure knowledge only He would know. We release His heart to others. That is what we do. About 2004, our ministry made a shift. Instead of us doing all the prophesying, we began to teach others how to prophesy. I was teaching and preaching in Lima, Peru, and ministry time came, as was usual for us. I had a team with me, which was also usual. The team began to prophesy, giving words to different people in the congregation. Many were blessed, changed, and brought closer to the Lord. Then it hit me: I'll pray for this one girl to prophesy to the entire congregation. I did, and she did! The new "hearer" began to prophesy to others in the congregation. God is so wonderful.

God's Voice is Transcendent over Culture

I go to African nations where the women and the men are, literally, divided by seating in the church buildings. We practice this equipping ministry in these places and I follow the leading of the Holy Spirit. Baptized by His glory and love, within a couple of days, the men and women are prophesying over each other. The cultural differences are pushed aside. The relegated roles for women are broken. Yes, maybe it's only for a time or a season. The behavioral pattern has to be broken and it may take a constant flow of the prophetic anointing before hardened traditions are broken. Yet, it's amazing to see what Papa's love can do and how the people respond to God's goodness and His amazing power. He is a big God!

Isn't that what happened during the time of Christ? Jesus talked to the unlovely, the prostitutes, tax collectors, "women," Samaritans, and the poor. The politics of Jesus can be characterized by radical obedience to His Father and His love. His apparent disobedience and flagrant civil disdain on the outside was really a passion driven by love and raw obedience to the Father.

I met Alfonso on my first trip to Sierra Leone. Apprehension seemed to be embedded upon his face as we met together with local pastors for a pastors' conference. I could tell Alfonso was unsure of what was about to take place. Having a multicultural prophetic team of twenty-something's in my entourage probably didn't help much. Faith is sometimes characterized by doing something so grand and large that if Papa doesn't show up, it will surely fail. I knew Alfonso, a local pastor, was a little concerned about the probability of this taking off. To be honest, so was I. I was about to teach in 90 degree heat for six hours a day, with constant attention as to how to speak, purposely avoiding offense to anyone, listening to Holy Spirit, and providing opportunities for the interns to be involved and grow in the ways of God. Wow, I see that now; I'm glad at the time that I was less than cognizant of all that was happening. But, God did show up! He always does.

Having arrived at our destination in Kambia, we had the evening free to eat dinner and hang around. In Africa, eating is an event, not a quick pick-up at a local restaurant. So, we had some real quality time together—unlike the four hour journey into Kambia on dirt roads with faces covered as we tried not to ingest too much of the red dirt. That night was the perfect time to get acquainted in the Holy Spirit.

We prayed with Alfonso with his permission. We spent about thirty to sixty minutes hearing God, speaking His words and watching Alfonso being mightily touched by the

Lord. It was noticeable to all that God was healing. All the walls were broken down when Papa showed up.

More walls were demolished the next day, the first day of the pastors' conference. Alfonso, leader of the group, began telling the story of what happened the previous night. Suddenly, I could understand many of his words spoken in Krio (a language with a lot of English words hidden within it). He said, "These people from America are truly prophets. They hear from God and they saw me as a little boy, running from a fire. Come, listen to the man of God; he is a prophet." That got everyone's attention, to say the least. They were ready to listen and learn how to do some of the same. Moreover, all who read these words today can do what I have been doing and more. "His sheep follow Him because they know His voice" (John 10: 4).

On another occasion in India, we were again holding a pastors' conference. Following our teaching and a few prophetic words, the Spirit of the Lord fell and all began prophesying. There was such a spirit of love there; we went about hugging one another and praying for one another. We washed each other's feet. The people knew we were for real. There are no boundaries that the love of Jesus Christ cannot overcome. To experience the width, length, height, and depth of the love of Jesus Christ is exponentially more impacting than talking about it! To know the power and hear the person of Jesus Christ is to have His love. To have ascertained His love is to know the power, and hear the voice, of the Shepherd.

Knowing His voice is to *know Him*. The supernatural voice of Papa quickly cut across cultural boundaries with the Samaritan woman (John 4). The harvest that comes from prophecy is beautiful. "Many of the Samaritans from that town believed in him because of the woman's testimony, 'He told me everything I ever did'" (John 4: 39).

KNOWING HIS VOICE IS TO *KNOW HIM*.

God's Voice is Transferable

We teach classes on how to hear God's voice. People who've never heard His voice before begin to hear. Every time! Every time! God wants His children to hear His voice and be captivated by His intimacy. This generation will know that hearing God is not just for the "greats," but for all. Prophecy is to be released, imparted, and transferred to this generation for all to hear His wonderful words.

Why? Because He Loves! You know this is Biblical, don't you? The mandate for all to prophesy is foreshadowed in Joel 2 and fulfilled in Acts 2: "In the last days, God says, I will pour out my Spirit on all people. Your sons and daughters will prophesy, your young men will see visions, your old men will dream dreams. Even on my servants…" (v. 17-18).

Paul then says to "follow the way of love and eagerly desire spiritual gifts, especially the gift of prophecy" (1 Cor. 14: 1). Everyone is admonished to prophesy, that is, to hear His voice and to speak His words in a loving way. We who are in the equipping ministry know that everyone can hear! (Eph. 4: 11-13)

During Lifegate's regular meeting times, we try to always allow time for Papa to speak to His people. Many times, we will prophesy over people or divide up and prophesy over one another. Once, I noticed a young woman holding back, not taking an active part, so I went to hang out with her. We talked for a while. Then I asked for permission to pray for her. She said yes and Papa had great things to say. Next, I asked her, "Can you pray for me?" She replied, "Well, I don't hear from God very well." I said, "Ok, let's try this together." "OK!" she exclaimed. I prayed with her again and asked her to look for a picture, or listen for a word or a thought that might pop in her mind. She began to give words over me. She was so amazed that she could hear God's voice.

Once I was praying with a guy for an extended period of time during one of our *LifeChanges*[1] prayer appointments. He told me up front that He didn't hear God very well. I said that was okay. After two and a half hours, he had gone to the heavens and heard God some fifteen times. He pointed out to me that heaven was loud. I said, sure, there's a lot of praise going on there. I later pointed this out because I knew he hadn't recognized it. He was slightly surprised to hear it put that way.

I was praying with a fifteen year old who had never heard from God. After praying for him about ten minutes, I asked if he heard or saw anything. He shouted, "Wind!" I said really? He said, "Yeah." I pointed out that sometimes in the Bible, wind shows the power and provision of God, even by His angels. He said, "Yeah." He acted fairly nonchalant in the moment. Later, through a series of events and prayer sessions, we found that he has been healed from many wounds and problems. Even his therapist noticed and reported positive changes in him.

The Spirit of prophecy is definitely transferable. Even King Saul was numbered among the prophets (1 Sam. 10: 11). Saul was changed into another person when the Spirit of the Lord came on him. Later, the Apostle Paul desired to impart gifts to the church, to transfer this wealth that had been given to him. God desires to transfer the wealth of power and anointing. The world is waiting for this transfer.

I was praying recently with a Muslim. We have had many talks, mainly about life and the challenges we face. Some things about God will come up, but not in some awkward, intentional, canned way. He was hurting emotionally one day and I asked if I could pray for him. He said, "Yes." After praying, he opened his eyes, giving a huge sigh, saying, "WOW!" I asked him what happened and he confessed that he really felt a presence he had never felt before. We went on to talk about the Kingdom. I pray right now that his wounds would be healed and he would be open to hear more about our Savior.

Many people in our city, state, and around the world have received an awesome touch by God. Now MORE is about to be released. Say "More, Lord" right now and see what God does! I've seen many come alive out of dark places through discernment, seeing visions, seeing the angelic, becoming the supernatural son or daughter of God they are created to be. God is releasing a powerful anointing around the world for His children to hear Him and get to know Him. Only those who are sipping from the same old well will miss out and miss Him. It's Papa's heart for you to know Him!

God's voice is Tactical

There is a reason and purpose in everything God does. With His voice, He desires to woo us closer to Him. This is how we get to know Him in intimate ways. In the church, we are to have a party with one another, abounding in the things that really matter: joy, peace, and righteousness (see Rom. 14: 17). Having said that, then we are to build up one another with words of life. "…everyone who prophesies speaks to men for their strengthening, encouragement, and comfort" (1 Cor. 14: 3). These are words that build up and bring joy to our spirit and soul.

See, Jesus is "Word" (John 1). Papa had so many things to say to His children that He named His firstborn (are you ready for this?) "WORD." That's right, *Word* is His name. So, He wants to speak to His people to bring "life!" He is the Way, the Truth, and the Life (John 14:6). Many people know Him occasionally as the *Way*. Many Christians know about Him as the *Truth*. But now God is calling YOU to know him intentionally as *Life*. He wants you to *know* everything about Him. He wants you to know Him and in the process, you begin to know yourself as He knows you. He wants you to know *who you are* and *what you are to do*. Enough of this floating around with a purposeless, hopeless life, living on the wrong side of the cross. He is the Resurrection and the Life and in Him is Life. He so wants to live with you, around you and through you at all times. Hearing Him is the gateway to life! "For the testimony of Jesus is the spirit of prophecy" (Rev. 19:10b). Whenever Holy Spirit shows up, there is prophecy. There are words. Wherever there are His Words, Jesus is in the room. Jesus brings words and they flow out of your mouth!

Just a thought, how will you ever get to know Him without hearing His voice? Recently, my wife lost her voice for about seven days. After about three days, I really began to miss her. After five days, I was lonely and really felt like she was no longer a part of my life. I didn't just miss her; she was no longer a part of "life." Our words bring life to each other. If you don't hear Jesus on a regular basis, "you are no longer a part of life." You may know Him as the "Way." You may know "Truth" about Him, but you do not know Him! It is time to get to know Him. That is why He left. Jesus said that it was good for Him to leave so that we would have Holy

Spirit. Sure, we get to do the things that we read in the "Truth" about Him, but He wants us to be able to hear the truth that is poured into us like new wine and fed to us like fresh bread that sustains us. He wants us to have *life*. Just knowing Him as the "Way" can become a routine that can get old in a hurry. Knowing Him as the "Truth" can become legalistic and shallow very quickly. But knowing Him as *Life* will always sustain our ever-changing needs and personalities. He created us to be multi-faceted and creative. That's why there are new songs, new mercies, new problems to solve, new solutions. Everyday is a new day with Him. It is *life* and it is *living*! Changing! Growing! Becoming like Him! I heard Jane Hamon put it like this one time in a conference:

> Prophetic people hear God; they hear the inaudible.
> Prophetic people hear God; they see the invisible.
> Prophetic people hear God; they believe the incredible.
> Prophetic people hear God; they think the unthinkable.
> Prophetic people hear God; they do the impossible.

Faith is exercised in hearing God. Once you have heard His voice, you can go to the ends of the earth knowing God is with you!! Receiving the tactical movements of God affords you the opportunity for pinpoint accuracy in the Kingdom of God. We simply ask, "Jesus, what do you want to say about this?" Gaining Kingdom initiatives for a person, a group, or a nation is paramount. God sent people on divine missions all the time. Just to name a few: Joseph (Gen. 45:5-8); Moses (Exod. 3:9-10); Nathan to David (2 Sam. 12:1); Paul and Barnabas (Acts 13:2-4); and He now sends you (Eph. 2:8-10). Yeah, He's dying, or shall we say, He died to send you on a divine mission in order to have a divine appointment covered and smothered with His divine love!

He wants to have this incredible love affair with you and take you on an exciting journey that brings forth a river of living water. He wants the River of Life to flow from His throne (see Ezek. 47) right into you to keep you in perfect peace with your eyes stayed on Him! He's after your heart! Have an epic journey! Let Him be your Vision and Purpose! You can't go wrong.

Oh Lord, release this Elijah Generation with your heart. Let us have an incredible journey with You!! Release the lions!

God's Voice is Tantalizing

I love this part!! Paul said to **"LUST"** after the greater gifts, like prophecy! No less than three times does Paul use the Greek word, *zaloute*, to describe one's passion. We are to "be zealous, covet, be addicted, or to lust after" this gift of hearing God: "But eagerly desire the greater gifts" (1 Cor. 12:31). Then he unveils the greater gift: "Follow the way of love and eagerly desire spiritual gifts, especially the gift of prophecy" (1 Cor. 14:1). What makes it so great? "Since you are eager to have spiritual gifts, try to excel in gifts that build up the church" (1 Cor. 14:12). Building up the church and doing the things of Jesus is more tantalizing than anything that the world has to offer. The enemy is so desperately trying to deceive the X, Y, and Z generations with lust after the things of this world. Paul was obviously wrestling with the same issues in the church of Corinth. Paul's message to us today is the same: replace the lust of this world with the lust of hearing God on a routine basis, building up the body and transforming the world.

Prophetic shorts: Most often, I go into a restaurant and ask Papa, "What do you want to say to my server?" He always has something to say. In one restaurant I asked and He impressed upon me a word about open fields and butterflies. Our server had just booked a vacation for Kansas just to run in the open fields. Her response was, "How did you know that?" Then I delivered Papa's heart for her and told her how beautiful she was. She cried. At a local Chili's, I received the word late so I ran after the server. I gave her the word, then others wanted to receive a word! I prayed for a cook in a Chinese restaurant; many came closer to Jesus that night. At an IHOP (the pancake house), I had the server lead in prayer. She ended up in tears. In another Chili's, I had a word for a server, then my wife had a word about her education. It goes on and on. Hundreds of times!!! Literally! An antique dealer in Asheville, a man at Blowing Rock, a guy on the Blue Ridge Parkway, a server at Fatz Restaurant in Franklin, NC. On and on it goes. Some of the most rewarding memories my wife and I have had on our little mountain trips are when Papa shows up and shows off. He does it every time.

Many will keep God in a doctrine! Many will quench the Holy Spirit by stigmatizing His gifts! The "love of God" can be argued over and against the gifts of the Spirit. (I say they go hand in hand.) The outpouring of Papa's heart was "so yesterday," some might say. The story of the Bridegroom and Bride is for Mike Bickle and company. The lukewarm, anemic, assertions continue, spiraling into a quagmire of illegitimacy and ultimate destruction. Many will miss life if they don't grab the absolute, experiential knowledge of Papa's love and this whole Bride and Bridegroom relationship. I WANT TO KNOW GOD AND THE POWER OF HIS RESURRECTION IN ME! (See Eph. 1.) You must repeat that over and over. The fifteen inches from your head to your heart is the longest distance in the world. Ask God to rock your world with His love. It will be a well that you will "lust" after. It is better than gold! It is more addictive than cocaine. It'll give you a real buzz! WARNING: THIS DRUG CAN BE ADDICTIVE! CALL DR. JESUS IF YOU EXPERIENCE ANY DIZZINESS OR DROWSINESS. DO NOT DRIVE ANY VEHICLE EXCEPT THE VEHICLE OF MINISTRY IN WHICH HE PLACES YOU! SHOULD YOU FIND YOURSELF CLINICALLY ADDICTED, ASK FOR MORE!

God's Voice is Transformational

Life, as we know it, will change forever as we live in the River of Life. The atmosphere will totally transform as we carry the Word that "encourages, strengthens, and comforts" (1 Cor. 14: 3). The positive Word of Christ will change any situation and dominate your life. Because of what Jesus has done on the cross and what He is doing to redeem your life, the prophetic word always builds up and encourages. The world today desperately needs to hear that. Things need to change, wherever you are, whatever you are doing.

Recently I was suddenly in charge of a conference, hosting about 250 to 300 people. In Snellville, Georgia, there are only one or two venues that can handle a group of that size except for a couple of churches. I needed to get a place NOW! I found a place that was open for the rapidly approaching dates and could accommodate our needs. The cost for the building to house the conference was going to be nearly $4000. I knew this was outside our budget, so after meeting with Bill (the owner of the building), I told him I would think about it and get back to him.

By the way, while I was talking with Bill about the building, I felt the presence of the Lord. I kept one foot in reality and one foot in the river. I was talking with my mind about the arrangements and our needs while I was speaking in tongues under my breath. As we were about to finish our meeting, I asked Bill if he was a Christian; I could sense that he was. Bill replied, "Yes, this is the way I do business—with God's help." I told him that I saw him at first with a guitar, but as I listened further to God's voice, I realized it was a keyboard. Bill's eyes welled up with tears and he said, jokingly, "Shut up, now you're getting too close!" I went on to tell him that God was going to put him back into worship and not just in a band or a group, but in worship. I told him he was created for worship. He kept saying, "Wow, my God. How did you…" I told him to hang in there, God isn't through with him. Needless to say, it was a powerful and transformational moment for Bill.

Meanwhile, I continued searching for a venue for the conference. I tried several churches to no avail. The following Sunday, I prayed with our church to bring the $4000 figure down to $2500. Impending time constraints were quickly coming and I needed to let Bill know something soon. On Monday afternoon, I texted Bill, trying to convince him to lower the total amount. We texted back and forth, then I got a partial text and then a phone call from Bill. He said, "Man, my thumbs and fingers froze up! I couldn't text you. I know this is God; this is the way I work! You can have the building for $2500." TRANSFORMATIONAL, I thought. Bill let us have the building and the room next to it for the $2500 amount. Praise God!

The power of the prophetic word can transform people; it can transform the atmosphere; it can transform your wallet. It changes lives, cultures, and nations. "The Word of God is living and active. Sharper than a double-edged sword, it penetrates even to dividing soul and spirit, joints and marrow; it judges the thoughts and attitudes of the heart" (Heb. 4:12). That Word is living in you and is active enough to bring forth transformation time and time again. God wants to use your tongue to change the world.

God's Voice is Transonic

The Word of God moves at the speed of information from His throne room to your spirit. Then, it moves out of your mouth at approximately 741 miles per hour. Anything above this speed is called supersonic. Transonic refers to the condition of flight in which a range of velocities of airflow exist surrounding and flowing past an air vehicle. Anytime it moves above the speed of sound, the transonic speeds that measure the movement of the vehicle (your words) against the air flow and condition of its environment may produce sudden wind shifts and shocks throughout the air making a supersonic loud noise. Correlating with the prophetic word, the words we say, zephyring out of the heavens, may cause such a shift and shaking that things change forever. Our tongues are powerful. Words move at transonic speeds.

"From the fruit of his mouth a man's stomach is filled; with the harvest from his lips he is satisfied. The tongue has the power of life and death, and those who love it will eat its fruit." (Prov. 18:20, 21)

"From the fruit of his lips a man enjoys good things…" (Prov. 13:2)

"He who guards his lips guards his life, but he who speaks rashly will come to ruin." (Prov. 13:3)

"The tongue that brings healing is a tree of life…" (Prov. 15:4)

"Do not let any unwholesome talk come out of your mouths, but only what is helpful for building others up according to their needs, that it may benefit those who listen." (Eph. 4:29)

"What goes into a man's mouth does not make him 'unclean,' but what comes out of his mouth, that is what makes him 'unclean.' " (Matt. 15:11)

"...say unto this mountain, 'Move from here to there,' and it will move..." (Matt. 17:20)

In years past, either I didn't have the understanding or the faith and experience to comprehend these passages. I thought of them as good Bible studies on how we "should" and "shouldn't" use our tongue. The idea of moving mountains was totally incomprehensible. James 3:1-12 and many passages in Proverbs speak about the tongue. These are not examples of how you speak when you ascertain some assent of the mind with knowledge gained by scholars. These are examples of having wisdom beyond worldly wisdom; wisdom that sets things in order and brings freedom to the captive. These are the Words of Jesus that transform the atmosphere.

Declarations are made throughout the Bible! David made them—not to hear himself speak; He spoke knowing the power of the tongue. Declarations are used in every area of life. Declarations are spoken in many ceremonies, whether in a church ordination, a wedding, or the inauguration of the President of the United States. In the United States of America, our forefathers penned a powerful document, the Declaration of Independence, which became foundational for our country. Words of declaration are powerful.

Just think about it. Jesus is the Word. He still speaks today; we are His sheep and we know His voice. We will do even greater things than Him (John 14:12). Then, "The testimony of Jesus is the spirit of prophecy" (Rev. 19:10b). We will overcome by our testimony (Rev. 12:11). The overcoming, powerful, encouraging, edifying Word of Jesus speaks through us and changes everything at supersonic and transonic speeds.

Jesus healed the demoniac with a spoken word, "Come out of this man" (Mark 5:8). He raised the little girl from the dead by a word, "Little girl, get up" (Mark 5:41). Jesus healed the paralytic, "Take up your bed and walk" (Luke 5:23). Peter spoke and healed the crippled beggar, "In the name of Jesus of Nazareth, walk" (Acts 3:6). These are only a few cases when Jesus just used the spoken word! If you think the power of Jesus' words were only for those times, not ours, I'm truly sorry. Please read Chapter One of this book and pray for God to reveal His power. If you don't think that you are worthy, then read Chapter Six on sonship. If you don't think we can do the stuff, then read the example of our time near Narasaraopet, India, and the waters rose 100 meters by the spoken word; or read my story regarding a plane in inclement weather—the Lord spoke through me and the weather cleared up. If you are saying right now, "Yeah, maybe you can do it, but I can't," then I would say go for inner healing and try faith in baby steps. Try declaring small things and watch Papa work miracles in your life.

Food for thought: genes and chromosomes are broken down to DNA. DNA has smaller strings of "genomes." These genomes are made up of "quarks." They have light, electric charge, and color. The most notable light is an unusual gold and white. Scientists have recently discovered that the strings of genomes and epigenomes can be changed by attitude. Your attitude can change your DNA. Your attitude is changed by the declaration of what God is saying over you. Therefore, THE DECLARATION OF THE PROPHETIC WORD HEALS AND CHANGES YOUR DESTINY![1]

Be the transonic voice that God has created you to be! Change! Transform! Create what Papa wants and desires. Hang around people who hear God and speak Papa's heart. Be a change agent. I ask Papa to release this prophetic voice inside of you, the voice that breaks the oaks and causes thunder in the sky. (Psalm 29:9; 68:33) Let that voice be in you. Oh, Lord, release that voice in this prophetic hour in this Elijah Generation!

While in Jamaica on a missionary trip with one of my daughters, David, a friend of mine, and I had a specific formidable task of trying to change the mindset of about a hundred young boys. Our assignment was to change a culture of boys who were predisposed to treat women badly, coupled with the daunting task to get them off the newfound pornography feed from the internet. We did a number of things that week, but I think a large portion of the transformation we saw came from the declarations that were made. We taught the boys and led them in declarations of identity, truth, and destiny as men of God. At the end of the week, the director of the camp wanted a copy of our "lesson." There was such a transformation in the boys and their treatment toward the girls that the director wanted to "teach" it again. It was challenging to explain the power of declaration to a cessationist culture. The boys had a whole new attitude. We spent time teaching, talking, and declaring truths about the sanctity of life. Women are a part of that sanctity of life. You may see some reflection of that in these declarations. I encourage you to begin making declarations over your life and the life of others.

See the CHANGE!

DECLARATIONS OF TRUTH

1. I am made in the image of God. (Genesis 1:27) I am fearfully and wonderfully made. (Psalm 139:3)
2. I am loved by my heavenly Father. He loves me even as He loved His son, Jesus. (John 17:23) It is His desire to lavish His love on me. (I John 3:1) His thoughts toward me are countless as the sand on the

seashore. (Psalm 139:17-18)

3. God's plans for my future has always been filled with hope. (Jeremiah 29:11) He is able to do more for me than I can possibly imagine. (Ephesians 3:20)

4. If I seek the Lord with all my heart, I will find Him. (Deuteronomy 4:29) If I seek His Kingdom and His righteousness first, then all that I need will be given to me. (Matthew 6:33)

5. I am the light of the world because the Light of the world lives in me. I will shine my light for the world to see. (Matthew 5:14) I will grow in your light and the understanding of who you are and who I am in you.

6. God's Kingdom will come and His will shall be done on earth as it is in heaven and it will begin in me. (Matthew 6:9-10) People will see me and know that I am a follower of Jesus.

7. The Holy Spirit is working in me to produce love, joy, gladness, peace, patience, kindness, goodness, faith-fulness, humility and self-control. (Galatians 5:22-25) I live and walk by the Spirit of God, having my conduct fully controlled by the Holy Spirit.

8. I have the same attitude, purpose and humble mind operating in me which is also in Christ Jesus. Jesus is my example of humility. I will serve others just as Jesus became a servant for my sake on the cross. (Philippians 2:2-8)

9. I am God's handiwork and workmanship. I have been created in Christ Jesus to do good works which God prepared in advance for me to do. (Ephesians 2:10) I will join in the work of the Father as He teaches me His ways.

10.   I walk together in peace and love with my brothers
and sisters in Christ. It is good and pleasant for us to
live together in unity. That unity brings a blessing
from the Lord. (Psalm 133)

Brigitte is a small village in Sierra Leone. I have been blessed to preach there under a "stick and limb lean-to" on several occasions. I remember the first time I preached in the church hut because of the red badge of courage I received. It was a bloody mark on my forehead caused when my head met a stick which supported the roof. My height had some bearing on that. More than that, however, I recall the warmth of the people and the results of declaring the Word to them and with them. This hut was a "preaching point" for Pastor Justus and many others to come and declare the Word. After many days, the harvest of those words were manifested. At least on two occasions, I have been privileged to baptize around thirty to forty people. We have helped build a church building there, moving from a hut to a sturdy building with no sticks to dodge. We have helped dig a well for the village. (Graciously, the Christians will now freely share the water with the Muslims, though in years past, many of the locals did not share water with Christians.) We've also built a primary school and an orphanage. Another building is being constructed to serve as a training center for area pastors to come and learn how to share Bible stories in remote villages. Since the illiteracy rate is so high, the people will tell the stories of Jesus over and over, from generation to generation. I believe declarations of His Word were tantamount for the coming of the Kingdom in this one small village in Africa.

"My sheep will know my voice," John records. Hearing God is a must for this Elijah Generation to do the exploits of Jesus. Then lambs will become lions.

1. Extrapolated from a message of John Paul Jackson and further examined through Wikipedia.

8

THE FATHER RELEASING HIS HEART

I HAD A DREAM. In the dream, I'm in a theater—a very crowded theater with lots of nationalities around me. Sitting next to me is a little girl about four or five years old. She stood up on her seat and began kissing me all over my face. This made some of the people around me a little uncomfortable. In fact, I was a bit on edge because of the apparent societal ramifications of a child kissing an older man. I didn't want anyone to assume it was improper, so I told everyone around me that this sort of thing happens to me all the time; and that it started about ten years ago and I can't stop it. I said, "Children come up to me all the time."

As I awakened, I thought about the dream. Parts of the dream were literal. Children do come up to me all the time; young ones and older ones. I'm reminded of the movie, *The Santa Claus*. Tim Allen plays the part of the Santa Claus newbie. Kids begin coming to him, getting closer and closer until they are in his lap, telling him their wish list. I've always wondered if Jesus was a bit like that. I wonder if He had some attraction about Him that children would stick to Him like a magnet. Children can spot real, sincere love. I wondered and secretly prayed, "I want to be like that." I wanted the molasses that would draw men to Jesus. God answers prayers.

My grandchildren love me! My family has noticed and remarked on the evident bond I have with our grandchildren; they just like to be with me. They seem to stick to me. One of my daughters laughingly, but pointedly, acknowledged, "Oh, it's the Father's Heart!"

Papa's heart, that is—His love, is available today to marinate you into a "sticky" person. People will come! Oh yes, they will come! You'll find yourself running just to get some quiet time with the Father, just like Jesus.

Where are the Fathers and Mothers?

I am so thankful for my two grandchildren. At the time of this writing, I have only two, but I'm sure I will have more in coming years. I had no direct influence in the selection of their names, but both of their names are derivatives of Elijah. That's ironic! No, it's prophetic! I believe it is a prophetic sign as I write this book and consider the direction of my life. It is a prophetic sign for the confirmation of the calling of this Elijah Generation and the calling of Fathers—for how can we have the children without the Fathers?

> See, I will send you the prophet Elijah before that great and dreadful day of the Lord comes. He will turn the hearts of the fathers to their children, and the hearts of the children to their fathers, or else I will come and strike the land with a curse.
> (Mal. 4:5-6)

Four hundred years later, we find John the Baptizer turning the hearts of the Father to the children and vice versa. Add a couple of thousand years, the call is still just as radical—for this generation to go forth with the same intensity and message. But how? Where are the fathers and mothers?

I often hear grumblings and excuses from forty and fifty year olds, "Well, all I ever hear is about how the younger generation is going to carry the torch. What about me?" Or, sometimes I hear the opposite side of the spectrum, "I'm just too tired; I'm okay where I am now." The purpose of the Father, however, never wanes and is continually calling to us, season upon season.

I have good news. Here is a sure four-point plan for a purposeful destiny:

1. Repent
2. Get under the anointing.
3. Allow the Lord to put a fire in your belly.
4. Release the Kingdom!

Repent from religion that only requires you to show up on Sunday morning. Repent from a mindset that puts miracles in a past millennia. Repent from a faith that gets you to heaven, but not strong enough to bring someone else with you. Repent from the hypocrisy of having a form of religion, but no fire. Repent from a dead faith that has no works. Repent from your past wounds, bitterness, and pride. Repent from abdicating your place in life to someone else. Repent from the lies of the devil who says you aren't the one—someone else should do it. (Look around you; you reap what you sow.) Maybe I'm a little hard right here, but let's go ahead and get this out! It's time to change! NONE of us want to go into our most productive years only to have said that we put 35 years in XYZ company. Things are really shaking right now in our world and that affords us a grand opportunity to bring forth the Kingdom—Papa's heart! Some of you should be Fathers and Mothers for the generations following you. It's time to be weaned from the milk of microwave religion and dig deeply into the treasures of heaven!

Get in the anointing. Yes, go to church, but that's not what I'm discussing here. GIVE ME REVELATION!!!! Only the revelation of Papa's love will cause us to respond with repentance and a relentless pursuit and release of the Kingdom. As I said in an earlier chapter, go find the anointing. Go find a church that will pray for you until... Go find a group of people that are determined to pray through in order to get results. Go find a group that has Papa's heart. Go get the revelation that will put a fire in your belly. Go find a revival. Go start a revival. Papa wants you to be a forerunner, a lion! He wants you to be an equipper to rebuild the ancient ruins. He wants you to be a carrier of His love, one who will repair the walls of salvation and the gates of praise and restore streets in which to dwell (see Isa. 58:12).

In the Old Testament when the *heart* is mentioned, its meaning wasn't broken into parts like it is now. The Greeks, among others, taught us how to separate man into a menagerie of compartments: mind, flesh, emotions, will, psyche, body, etc. God made us to be one holistic person, beautifully transmitting His light, love and life. As He transforms us by His Love, the salvation of Jesus Christ, and the power of His Spirit, we somehow attain this fire in our belly, this destiny in our knower. Our fire burns for all the world to see.

Pray for the Lord to release you into a land that needs to hear and see what Papa has put inside of you. This book is a tablet of stories. When I was living out these stories, I didn't know what I know now. I only used what Papa put inside me. It was a fire that burned out of control and even without wisdom at times but, praise God, I had a fire! You may be set free tomorrow to preach "the Kingdom of God is at hand," or it may take some time to see the fullness of His promise in you. But whatever you do, do quickly. Begin now! Burn now! I pray alongside the Christians in the book of Revelation, "Come quickly, Lord! Come quickly."

Releasing the Father's Heart

To have an experience without a Biblical basis is counterproductive or, at worse, cultic. To know Him is to experience Him; but some might ask, "How do you know it's Jesus?" Do we rely totally on experience? Hence, let's look at the Scriptures for the true nature of God. That is, let's look at the Father's Heart: Love!

99 ATTRIBUTES OF THE FATHER'S HEART

Papa is Love	1 John 4:7-8
He is Omnipotent	Rev. 19:6
He is Omnipresent (He knows where I am.)	Ps. 139:7; Ezek. 48:35
He is Omniscient (He knows my thoughts.)	Ps. 139; Rev. 22:13
He is not bound by Time	Isa. 44:6
God is Good and no evil is in Him	1 John 1:5
He is Pre-existent	Gen. 1:1-3
He is Transcendent above Nature	Heb. 1:3
He has a Personality	1 John 4:7-8
He is a God of Order	Isa. 45:18-19
He is Creator	Gen. 1:26-27
He only Creates Good	Gen. 1:31
He is Gregarious	Song of Sol. 4:1-15
He is Redeemer	1 John 4:10

He is Salvation	1 Cor. 15:45-49
He is Righteousness	Rom. 1:17;
	Jer. 23: 5-6
He is Judge over our enemies	Ps. 98:9
He is over History	Rev. 5:9
He is the Restorer	Ps. 23:3;
	Mal. 4:6
He is Healer	Isa. 53:5
He is a Shepherd	John 10:14
He is Peace	Judg. 6:24
He is Unchanging	Mal. 3:6
He is the Christ	Matt. 16:16;
	Luke 9:20
He is the Provider	Gen. 22:8, 14
He is the Breath of Life	Job 33:4
He is the Bread of Life	John 6:35
He is the Mighty Warrior	Exod. 15:3
He is the One who Sees	Ps. 11:4
He demonstrates Power over Nature	John 6:16ff
He is Holy	Isa. 43:3
He is our Intercessor	Rom. 8:27
He is the King of kings	Rev. 19:16
He is Faithful	Phil. 2:13
He is the God of the Most High	Deut. 10:17-18
He is the All Sufficient One	Gen. 28:3;
	Exod. 3:13-14
He is Daddy	Rom. 8:14
He is Lord	Exod. 6:2
He is Understanding	Job 32:8
He is Father	Matt. 23:9
He performs Signs	Exod. 10:2
He speaks Face to face	Num. 12:8

He is Truth	John 16:13
He Hears	Mal. 3:16
He is the Doorway	John 10:9;
	John 14:6
He is the Giver of visions and dreams	Acts 2:17
He is the Giver	John 3:16
He gives us His Holy Spirit	John 15:26
He is the Giver of perfect Gifts	Jas. 1:17
He is Word	John 1:1;
	Rev. 19:13
He Speaks	John 10;
	Isa. 52:6
He is the Giver of Revelation	1 Cor. 2:10
He is always Speaking	Ps. 19:1-4
He is the Bridegroom	Rev. 19:7; 22:17
He announces New Things	Isa. 42:9;
	John 16:13
He Dances and Sings over you	Zeph. 3:17
He is Close to the Brokenhearted and Saves	Ps. 34:18
He is Made Known through Visions	Num. 12:6
He Knows my Name	Ps. 139:1;
	Isa. 43:1
He Creates no mistakes	Ps. 139:13-16
He is Power	Acts 1:8
He Speaks in the Night	Num. 12:6
He is the Beloved that pursues His bride	Song of
	Sol. 2:4ff
He is the Spirit of Knowledge and	Isa. 11:2;
Understanding	1 Sam. 2:3
He is a Strong Tower	Prov. 18:10
He is the Restorer	Ps. 51:12; 23:3;
	Nah. 2:2

He is Joy and Strength	Neh. 8:10
He touches His children, like a Father and a Mother	Mark 10:13ff
He blesses His Children and takes them in His arms	Mark 10:16
He will not treat us as Orphans	John 14:18
He makes His Home with us	John 14:23
He releases the Mother's heart with comforting breast	Isa. 66:11
His Mother's heart has abundant breast milk	Isa. 66:11b
His Mother's heart: you will nurse	Isa. 66:12
His Mother's heart: you will be carried on her arm	Isa. 66:12b
His Mother's heart: you will be dandled on her knees	Isa. 66:12c
His Mother's heart: you will be comforted	Isa. 66:13
His Mother's heart: your heart will rejoice	Isa. 66:14
His Mother's heart: you will flourish	Isa. 66:14b
His Mother's heart: Gentle	1 Thess. 2:7
His Mother's heart: Caring	1 Thess. 2:7b
His Mother's heart: Transparency, complete openness	1 Thess. 2:7c
He Heals our Wounds	Jer. 30:17
He gives us a Future and a Hope	Jer. 29:11ff
He exercises Kindness, Justice, and Righteousness	Jer. 9:24b
He Whistles: Nature and His Redeemed ones Come	Isa. 7:18; Zech. 10:8
He is a God to be Feared. He is Awesome!	Isa. 8:13
He is the God of "Yes"	2 Cor.1:19. 20; Jer. 32:17, 27
His Promises are "Yes and Amen"	2 Cor. 1:20

He is the God of "Omni-possible"	Phil. 4:13; Mark 10:27
He moves Mountains	Matt. 17:20
He will Never Stop doing Good to you	Jer. 32:40
He will Answer you with Unsearchable Truths	Jer. 33:3
He is Yahweh (Everything)	Jer. 33:2b
He is the God of long arms and Strength to Rescue	Isa. 50:2
He has Powerful Words	Isa. 50:2c; Job 40:9
His Word is "Omni-sharp"	Heb. 4:12; Luke 1:37, 38
He is Jealous to Give us His Word and Spirit	Acts 2:17ff
He is our Encourager	2 Thess. 2:16-17

As I mentioned earlier, Candy and I have led over 1000 prayer sessions. We evangelize the heart by bringing the child of God closer to the Father. Sometimes Papa is so real and so close, we release more of His heart with an embrace. Candy will hug the person and then I will do likewise. Before our eyes, little lambs become mighty lions. We know the Father heart of God and the Mother heart of God are transferred through the hugs. We love to hear His children roar after such a God encounter! We sometimes roar with them, like the Lion of the Tribe of Judah might roar. The Father Heart of God is imparted prophetically and spiritually. The fire and roar, in all of our very beings, have to be released. The experience, the impartation, and the act of faith are culminated in what Papa has put in us and we give it away. It is love.

It is such a blessing to have Candy by my side as we minister. She truly has the Mother heart of God. People that have never bonded with their mothers may have pain that leads to addictions, compulsions, trust issues, fear of bonding, anxieties, fear of living, etc. Candy will pray, counsel, and impart rest, comfort, nurture, affection, trust, and intimacy. There is an event and a process. There are always immediate results during these prayer times with Papa, but then comes the reality of walking it out or living the truth. We help people learn how to walk in the truth of the new revelation they experienced (event) with God as they begin choosing new patterns of living (process).

When the heart of the Father is transferred as the tenderness of the lamb, the roar of the lion is manifested. We teach the new cub to look within, to look up, and to look around. As the warrior looks within, he or she sees the forgiving blood of Jesus at work. "Search me, O God," Psalms 51 states. For "Who shall ascend to the hill of the Lord, he who has clean hands and a pure heart" (Ps. 24:4). He begins to know who he is in Christ Jesus by looking up and laying hold of a new, true identity. Then, by looking around, he sees the enemy and what he's doing. The young lion finds a den in which to receive nurture and equipping—a safe place to learn and grow.

What then? We go out! We've received the Father's Heart to give it away! We are anointed to anoint others. We are smeared to smear the oil of gladness and the gospel of peace on other people. The manna will turn to maggots if we try to store it in a jar. Life, by its very nature, never lives until we give it away. What a blessing it is to be used by God! To know that you are really making a difference brings a new definition to life. I know the temptation is to settle for mediocrity. I believe we are arriving in a day that if we aren't constantly supplying oil for our lamps, our lights will go out. The sad thing is that many of our lights have gone out and we don't even know it.

WE'VE RECEIVED THE FATHER'S HEART TO GIVE IT AWAY! WE ARE ANOINTED TO ANOINT OTHERS.

YOU WERE CREATED FOR THIS! You are a father to someone and you are being fathered by someone. Release what you know to be truth in your spirit. Don't hold back. Give it away today and ROAR!

Wacky Theology or a Glorious System

I was a youth minister decades ago and served under some dynamic, powerful speakers. For a period of time, I sat under this bright young preacher who had a silver tongue. He was really good. It was amazing how quickly he could prepare a sermon. However, I saw several inconsistencies. He would use Scripture to fit his need for the moment. His theology would seem to change on one point or another so he could support his theme in a sermon. I would notice the inconsistencies and it troubled me. I didn't want to judge him, but I was propelled to strive toward a consistent theology rather than using Scripture to make my theology seem correct for the moment.

I had an Old Testament professor in college who frequently and admittedly misquoted Shakespeare with, "Consistency, thou art a jewel." This seemingly erroneous quote stuck with me. Consistency is a jewel and a rare jewel at that. So this "Father's Heart" stuff has really got to make sense across the board. If God is love and He has our best interests in mind all the time, then His love and goodness have to be true in every situation.

Can one actually create a paradigm, a foundational stone, from which all matters of ministry and doctrine might flow? Is this really what Papa was going for throughout the Bible, and even the ages? Is it really simply about relationship? Can all other teachings, prophecies, ministry, and the like, flow from and end up at the Father's Heart? Can His Love be the beginning and the ending of everything we do? Some reading this now might say, "Well sure, stupid, don't you get it?" It's all about Love! I mean really, it's just that simple, isn't it?

NOT SO FAST! What about evil? What about suffering? What happens when God doesn't heal? If God wants us to only prophesy good things out of His heart, then what about the Old Testament prophets? What about principles, faith teachings, and the Ten Commandments? How do these relate to the Father's heart? However complex these issues may be, I believe these issues, and more, can be resolved.

Papa's Love and Suffering

I have to raise the obvious question, if God loves us so, then why do we encounter suffering? Last night, I spent an hour talking to a guy who has been jettisoned forward at transonic speeds. His place in the Lord has been truly widened. I officiated his marriage to his bride just six months ago. Oops! She got pregnant right away. After encountering that unexpected surprise, they lost their baby at twenty weeks! It was hard. It was awful. As I talked with him, my heart was moved; there has to be some consistency in the theology of God's character. I just cannot comprehend Papa doing this!

He did not cause the baby to die so that they might somehow grow in character. The devil did it. The fall of man did it. But Papa is waiting at the banquet eating table with delicacies of restoration! God knows what the enemy is up to and He always plays His hand to a tee. Papa always is there to restore and renew, bringing us to a place where we know God better. When He restores, we become more like Him!

I don't have all the answers. I just know that suffering is with us always. And where life meets death, God is the author of life. Papa uses suffering to carve out a reservoir of His Presence that no one can rob, steal, or destroy. The enemy may come in and rob you of the externals, but Papa wants to put His territory, His Kingdom, His land, and His love in you so deep that you will become a wellspring of life for many to receive!

In every place the enemy wants to kill, steal, and destroy, Papa knows exactly how to "flip it" for our good. God allows and uses it for our good, every time! He cannot be God without bringing forth restoration! Let me say that again! By the very nature of who Papa is, He has to bring restoration; you're not just as strong as before, but actually stronger! You don't become a better person! You become more like God! The evidence of His supernatural glory living in you becomes more like that of a true son. You become like Jesus "who…made Himself nothing…therefore God exalted Him" (Phil. 2:6-11). It's never for worse; it's always for better.

I could site numerous examples from the Bible to support God's faithfulness to bring restoration out of trial and difficulty. They are quite obvious. Joseph was in the pit for thirteen years. Paul suffered and his were the marks of an apostle. Stephen, Abraham, and Moses experienced suffering and difficulty. We could go on and on creating a theology of suffering, believing one may need to suffer before being used by God. The problem with that is we often linger there too long and become self-made martyrs, crying in our beer, living as dysfunctional members in the body of Christ. But I have good news: the bad news is wrong! Wherever I find myself, the truth is that God is good and the enemy is bad. I will function in life, liberty, light, and love today! I'm at my best today, though tomorrow will be even brighter. God is always positive and I am free to serve Him today! Papa's heart is for me NOW!

Papa's Heart ad Godly Principles

I hope you can follow me here, but I really have a hard time teaching good solid Biblical principles in a vacuum. I so appreciate what the "Word of Faith" people teach. I really do! At this very moment, I am discovering a potpourri of keys in the Kingdom of Heaven. But if I'm not careful, I will wander off the path and begin practicing religion and not relationship. Every time I do this, there is a real check in my spirit. Principle without the Person of Jesus Christ is like eating week-old toast with no jelly. It's like eating stale saltines with no peanut butter or cheese. When you choose principle over the Person, you miss the point! You miss the real purpose behind the principle. As some might say, "You have to keep the main thing, the main thing—and the main thing is Jesus."

The principles work for awhile. I like "calling things that are not, as though they are" (Rom. 4:17b). Believe me, I do this everyday so my spirit will rise up to Papa's will and destiny in my life. I release my faith and the Kingdom! I teach our church these things. I make declarations. However, somewhere we have to sit at Jesus' feet and hear what He is saying. We have to continually know him on a day-to-day basis or we might just be speaking to the wind. What is your will, Papa? What do you say? If we opt for principle without the Person, we're just doing verbal exercises. Our souls are strengthened by declaring His principles. That is good for the moment. But I desire a rifle approach declaring God's will over my life and land instead of randomly shooting a scatter gun, possibly hitting the target every once and awhile. Again, the "Word of Faith" teachings are great. I desire these teachings. Praise God, they fit the paradigm of the "Father's Heart." With His love and Presence, we hit the target rather than straying into religion.

God, Biblical principles, axioms, and even the Ten Commandments are the guard rails that lead us to Jesus. Our nature cries out for these boundaries and keys. We wail for the rails! We do follow these proverbs and adages, for they lead us to Jesus. "So the law was put in charge (some translations: as a schoolmaster or guardrails) to lead us to Christ..." (Gal. 3:24). Following doctrine, principles, and the Ten Commandments is good, but the better is a relationship with the Person, Jesus Christ. If we **turn the page** in the Bible to Galatians 3:26 we read, "You are all sons of God through faith in Christ Jesus." If we **turn the page** again we read, "Because you are sons, God sent the Spirit of His Son into our hearts, the Spirit who calls out, 'Abba, Father'" (Gal. 4:6).

I heard a well-known minister give a wonderful message on "faith" and declaring the "Word." It was a great message, sharing the nuances of hope and love. This minister said hope was the positive expectation of something God was doing. Hope takes us to faith. It was also stated that if you don't have love, you have to go back and study it. YOU HAVE TO GO BACK AND STUDY LOVE? I submit to you today, like Paul, if you don't have love, you are just a "resounding gong or a clanging cymbal" (1 Cor. 13:1). Now, I am not criticizing the message, but I am offering a critique of any doctrine or teaching that is not firmly rooted in His love. It's not an "either/or," but a "both/and." We desire both the principles of faith and the substance of love. You can't get love by studying it. It comes from His Presence.

Faith without works is dead, but you'll die without His love. Without his Presence, we'll burn out. The test of your mettle is not how great you were at keeping house like Martha, but sitting at His feet and getting instruction like Mary. If we sit long enough at His feet, we'll get instruction. Those Kingdom initiatives are vital and are so rewarding in this life and the life beyond as we abound in relationship with Him.

Papa's Heart and Prophecy

As cited in earlier chapters, "But everyone who prophesies speaks to men for their strengthening, encouragement and comfort" (1 Cor. 14:3). We teach that the foundation of prophecy is hearing Papa's heart and encouraging one another with His message. However, there have been some who just don't understand that concept. It is surprising how people can give such sour, bitter, and vile prophecies and say it is God. They say, "Look at the Old Testament! You will see how God judged the earth and nations with His words." Therefore, I am forced to see if the message of the Father's Heart and a foundation of His love can coincide with the entire Bible.

I have also noted that I have traversed the world, teaching and preaching a message of Papa's heart—that He wants us to hear Him and have relationship with Him. To prophesy, simply put, is to hear the Father and say what He is saying. I'm always amazed to see people begin to not only hear God, but to prophesy to other people, encouraging, edifying, and comforting. What also amazes me is how many pastors and churches have been harmed by prophecy; I just didn't have a clue. Usually one of two things has happened. Either people in the unredeemed places of their hearts try to control the pastor and the people, or they unleash a hatred and judgment that is hurtful to the church and even to God. Consequently, the prophetic is usually just shut down and the church has nothing to do with it. Prophecy becomes a "dirty word" with a "taboo" mindset surrounding it. How unfortunate to shut down the voice of God!!

The continual quest is to rectify the naysayer with the positive power of the Holy Spirit. Let us rectify and qualify some of the formidable prophecies of the Old Testament, beginning with a Biblical principle which is dripping with Papa's heart: "Mercy triumphs over Judgment" (Jas. 2:13). "Blessed are the merciful, for they will be shown mercy" (Matt. 5:7). "I desire mercy, not sacrifice" (Matt. 12:7).

Mercy triumphs over judgment even in the Old Testament. He is the same God today, yesterday, and tomorrow. Father didn't receive the effects of Jesus Christ in the New Testament, we did. Father was the cause! He already had enough love to give us His Son. He had it in the Old Testament. Let us observe:

- Jonah prophesied, "Forty more days and Nineveh will be overturned" (3:4). Turn the page in your Bible and you will see how the people repented and God relented. Jonah was even angry at God because of His "compassion, slow to anger, and abounding in love" (4:3).

- Micah speaks against Samaria and Jerusalem in Chapters 1 and 2, but **turn the page** and you will see Papa's Heart of deliverance that is to come (3:12ff) and His establishment of the Mountain of the Lord where many nations will say, "Let's go up to the mountain of the Lord" (4:2). In fact, in the book of Micah, every time you observe the judgment of the wicked, **turn the page** and you'll see God's mercy, forgiveness, and call for repentance.

- Ezekiel 35 and 36 are words of judgment against Edom and Israel, but **turn the page** and you'll see how God will "look with favor" towards you (36:9) and He will give us a "new heart" (36:26). Even the Father's Heart for the Valley of Dry Bones was "to put my Spirit in you and you will live..." (37:14).

- Ezekiel's prophecies are harsh, but look at Papa's true divine plan. You have to read on and **turn the page** to discover the new temple (Chapter 40) and the glory returning to the temple (44:4). Literally, the temple is rebuilt; figuratively, the River of God is inside us (47:1-12).

- If you have the propensity to camp at the polluted river of judgment, you'll miss the main message of Isaiah. Sure, there is judgment in Chapter 10, but **turn the page** to Chapter 11: "a shoot will come up from the stump of Jesse and the Spirit of the Lord will be upon Him" (verse 1ff). Read the judgment of Isaiah 34, then **turn the page** to Isaiah 35, "there will be streams in the desert," "be strong and do not fear, He will come and save you!" Again, there is judgment against Assyria. Yet in the midst of the macro, Papa is concerned about the individual, Hezekiah (Chapter 38), and hears his prayer. Read Isaiah 40: "You will fly like eagles with wings."

- In the book of Jeremiah, there are multiple prophetic pictures, journeys, and acts. Some are a bit negative.

Turn the page. Chapters 29 – 31 are chocked full of memorable passages like, "I have a future and a hope for you" (29:11; 31:17). "Call on me and I will answer…" (33:3). "Is there anything too hard for me" (32:27). Don't you love Lamentations 3:22-23, "His mercies…are new every morning."

Quite literally, I could go on like this. I have gone through my Bible and have underlined all the positive decrees and words of the Lord. My Bible has been inked up! You show me an Old Testament prophet and I'll show you one with Papa's heart, if you only **turn the page**. It's funny how we sometimes find what we are looking for; sub-consciously we might be looking for a God to fit our negative experience of life. Because we have been wounded deeply, we feel there has to be some reason and we often blame God instead of the enemy. Sounds like a diabolical plan to me.

Sometimes I hear people prophesy, but they just don't know Papa. (See Matt. 7:22.) There are many who tell us how bad it's going to get. There are many who want to rail against the United States without speaking Papa's heart. Many prophet wannabes come in disjointed from the body, wounded and crusty, needing a platform to spew out a caldron of jaded speculations. I won't have it. It has to be stopped. Wounded people wound people and, as a pastor, I have to protect the flock from both corporate and individual prophecies. We have to know those who minister around us.

Prophecy is not prophecy until you know Papa's Heart! Without the true representation of Papa's heart, you are only discerning what is happening in someone else's life or, perhaps, what is going on in your own life. Prophecy is only prophecy when you hear Papa's heart of love coupled with a plan of redemption and the full assurance of restoration.

Therefore, we teach, train, and impart Papa's heart of comfort, strength, and encouragement. We teach people to "flip it" or to "**turn the page.**" Resting in the assurance of knowing the character of Papa, leaving doctrines and principles behind, we positively, unswervingly, and without reservation tell people to "flip it" to the positive. Even negative dreams are interpreted in the same manner as we "flip it" to see Papa's heart in the matter.

The best example of this is Jesus with the woman at the well (John 4). He didn't leave her with negative words, condemning her for having five husbands; He whet her appetite with Papa's heart: "…the water I give will…[be] a spring of water, welling up to eternal life" (vs. 14). To hear Papa's voice and deliver His message, always be ready with words of life that cut through the soul, dividing all other issues, and bring life, light, and love.

Papa's Heart and Spiritual Warfare

While in Africa, I met a pastor who seemed to be schooled in spiritual warfare. I would watch him bind and loose every spirit imaginable before each meeting. I could see his heart was in the right place, but I was concerned about the execution. I couldn't place my finger on it, but something seemed off. I later was able to help him see how the heavenly Father helps us in spiritual warfare. Notice that even Daniel prayed for twenty-one days for help in order to take on the big guys. I encouraged this pastor to do the same thing while trying to tackle principalities. I'm sure he had been taught that, however, I could also see how he would naturally attack the enemy with his prayers. Coming from a Muslim back-ground of law and a culture of witchcraft, it seemed that he just exchanged one set of incantations for another. Where there were certain sayings and statements used in witchcraft, he could easily deduce that Scripture could and should be used that way.

Don't we do the same thing? Many of us have used the Bible to try to cast out demons and principalities. As a result, we often got our tails kicked. We have unwittingly used the Bible as a book of incantations to do warfare, heal the sick, have church, and many other things that may or may not have gained results.

Turn the page to the relationship: "Father, what do you want to do here?" we might ask. What is the Father's Heart? What is He saying here? What are His Kingdom initiatives? I never knew that warfare could be fought while worshiping. If you find out that your intercession has become anemic, try worshiping and praising Him. You may find that others see an effervescent glow around you because you've been in His glory. Demons will flee in His Presence. Fasting, spiritual mapping, pulling down strongholds, prayer walking and terraforming, concerts of prayer, and the like will take on a whole new meaning. Coming from the foundation of Papa's heart and His voice is huge. The results could be explosive! Operating from the Father's Heart might really become a lifestyle we are ready to embrace.

Papa's Heart and Spiritual Gifts

"Something has to be done," Paula said with tears streaming down her face. While resolute in spirit, her emotions had gripped her as she watched her daughter, Faith, struggle with an intense bout of malaria and typhoid fever. Rick and Paula, missionaries in Sierra Leone, had counted the cost; however, this relentless attack on their child was too much!

After seeing the pain on their faces, I felt their heart's cry. I prayed and I felt Papa's heart. His love was overwhelming! It seemed that Papa and I were on the same frequency. My will resonated with His will. I asked, "Father, what do we do?" He said to go in and pray, so I did. He gave me a song to sing over Faith. Then Papa gave me a Scripture or two to read over her. I prayed again. I anointed her with oil. I did everything the Father told me to do. Just as Jesus only did what He saw His Father doing (John 5:19), I did the same. I received the "Kingdom initiatives" from above and obeyed them. Faith was healed. God did the work; I was merely the facilitator.

I'm convinced anything can be done if we wait on the Lord and receive His instructions. Most of the time, we ascertain our spiritual gift mix from inventories or tests, other people's observations, and prophetic words. These are all to be applauded. I often use these instruments; they are excellent avenues in the path to God and His Kingdom. Learning what we are to be about and how we fit into His Kingdom is huge! We need to know our spiritual gifts—who we are, how we tick, our strengths and weaknesses, our personalities—and utilize other self-actualization tests.

Moreover, can we **turn the page** from tools to relationship? What if we had a limitless Father that is bigger than our thoughts, our ways, our walls and even our gifts? Yes, His thoughts are bigger than our thoughts, His ways bigger than our ways. He wants to stretch us and fill us more and more, whereby, we do exploits we didn't know we could do. Full of faith and His Spirit, we do things we didn't even know we were capable of doing! Busting out of our pre-determined box, we listen, lean in, and let go the Kingdom of Heaven.

Hence, spiritual gifts and the Father's Heart become less about me and what I have control over to more about Him. We decree and declare, "Bring your Kingdom on earth as it is in Heaven" (Matt. 6). So, Father, use me to bring your Kingdom, everyday, all the time. Get me out of my box. I'm no longer a lamb, but a lion, ready to roar at the enemy. Do now whatever you want to do; use whatever spiritual gift that is in me to bring your glory and power to the earth.

The book of Acts is undoubtedly the most extraordinary book in the Bible. There were more of God's people doing more of God's miracles than ever before; it wasn't just regulated to a few. As history moved farther and farther away from Acts 2 & 10 (Holy Spirit encounters), the church began to synthesize, analyze, scrutinize, and criticize what the Holy Spirit wants to do and how He does it. Now we homogenize "it" so it is palatable to all. We "dumb down" the power of the Holy Spirit so that "it" will be acceptable to all. We even see this just a few years after the powerful coming of the Holy Spirit. Paul analyzed the work of the Holy Spirit and discussed the gifts within a decade of Pentecost. It's apparent that Paul never purposed to achieve these power gifts without the source. Papa's heart, love, and power transcends our control (and self-limitations) of our gifts. Relationship is paramount to a well thought-out religion!

We pray for revival. We seek another power awakening! We listen for a mighty rushing wind like Acts 2, but until He comes again with that power breakthrough, set your "eyes like flint" toward Jesus. Set your default button to always know Him, always seek Him, always do His will. Over the last few generations, "doing the will of God" has been laced with negative connotations of self-sacrifice and denial. Papa's heart is really the impetus for doing His will. His will is fun, full of discovery, loving, exciting, adventurous. Along the way, our flesh becomes worthless and we recognize that truth. We see that His way is so much more glorious than our self-seeking ways. And glory we will see! I want to know Him and His ways. I'm addicted. I want to become a lion—NOW! Yes, NOW! My understanding of my spiritual gifts is no longer limiting God! I want to do whatever God wants to do, whenever He wants! There is no longer a self-imposed ceiling over my aspirations. Lion of the tribe of Judah, roar over me!

Papa's Heart and Life!

When you come to the rudimentary essence of matter, you find a positively charged proton with negatively charged electrons swirling about. Such is life and the essence of God. God is for us and not against us, the Scriptures tell us. He is the Father who sings over us, or dances over us. He is the "Yes" and "Amen." All things are "Yes" in Christ Jesus.[1] To love Him with all our heart is the "yes" or the positive spirit in us. To love our neighbor is the "yes" or the positive love transferred to others. When I say "yes" to the law of love, then I say "no" to the negative things always swirling around me.

There are many no's in our lives. Elijah prayed for rain. As he sent his servant to check on the condition of the atmosphere, six times he got a "no." Then on the seventh time, he got a "yes" in the form of a cloud coming about the size of a man's hand (1 Kings 18:44). Afterwards, Elisha stayed at a house so much that the homeowners built a prophet's house for him next door. Later, the son—who was birthed by the prophet's earlier declaration—died and the woman mounted a horse to go find the prophet. She rode and rode, for she knew there was a "yes" waiting for her.

When asked how she was doing, she responded, "All is well." His servant asked, "How's your husband?" She said, "All is well." "How's your son?" "All is well." THEN, Elisha sent his servant to heal the boy with his staff. There was a "no," for the boy was not healed. He put the staff on the boy's face. Again, there was a "no." Elisha then came to the house: "no." Elisha prayed and there was another "no." He got up and laid upon the boy; the boy got warm, but still no healing. Elisha walked back and forth, still a "no." Then, Elisha laid upon the boy again, and finally there was a "yes" (2 Kings 4).

How many no's do we have to hear before we give up on Papa's love? His love always leads us to victory, restoration, or even a deeper revelation to His ways. Elisha just had to do the right Kingdom initiatives in order to release Papa's will. Elisha later healed Naaman of leprosy after instructing him to dip in the Jordan River seven times. The children of Israel marched around Jericho six days and then on the seventh, they marched seven times. There were many "no's," but one powerful yes. Even Jesus didn't heal much when there was little faith (Matt. 13:58). He got a no, but many more yeses.

HIS LOVE IS SO POWERFUL, SO POSITIVE, SO PURPOSEFUL, SO PERSONAL, SO PRACTICAL. HIS "YES" IN US BECOMES THE REALITY OF LIFE.

When we receive and understand His revelation, being continually filled with His Presence (because we leak out), then we will see the God of "Yes" manifest over and over. HOW DO WE GET THERE: by saying "Yes!" The "yes" in our spirit becomes one with the "yes" in Papa! HE IS "YES!" His love is so powerful, so positive, so purposeful, so personal, so practical. His "yes" in us becomes the reality of life. His "yes" is the testimony of Jesus living inside us!

Become a "yes man" with Papa and you will see Him manifest everyday! Life becomes a positive walk! Just because you get a no, it doesn't mean you should stop pursuing His "yes."

Papa's Heart and Systematic Theology

Creating an ecosystem with "Papa's Heart" is our vision. In our society, the electronic giant "Apple" has been colossal at creating a culture that transcends the reaches of imagination. Facebook and other companies are sure to follow. Is it not within our reach to create a culture of "Papa's Heart" within our context? In our milieu of the neighborhood, nations, and the next generation, is it time to ask our Creator how to share the width, breadth, heighth, and length of the love of Jesus Christ? Will this move of God continue so that "the earth will be filled with the knowledge of the glory of the Lord..." (Hab. 2:14).

Become a lion today!
Create a culture of Jesus, where ever you go!

---

1. Read: Phil. 4:13; Luke 1:37; Mark 10:27; 2 Cor. 1:20; Isa. 50:2; Job 42:2; Jer. 32:17, 27; 1 Sam. 14:6; Ps. 18:29; Matt. 17:20; 19:26; Mark 9:23.

BECOMING A LION

The Conclusion or, rather, the Beginning

Before writing this conclusion, I was sitting in a local restaurant eating by myself, asking Papa what He wanted to say to bring this book to a close. Suddenly, "practice what you've been saying" came to mind. Well, it hit me to just ask Holy Spirit what He wanted to do here. "Let Your Kingdom come." Quickly, a variety of Kingdom possibilities came into the room. I knew someone with health issues would come in and he did, carrying his oxygen tank. Then I heard the word "joy" (Isa. 61) and that a divorce had taken place, but a new person was coming into this woman's life. I thought I'd stay on the side of the prophetic since I didn't get a sense of healing in the room.

Pondering these things in my heart, I finished my meal. I knew I would come in contact with my waitress along the way to the exit and I could give her these words. I told her what I saw: "I see bright and yellow sunshine coming your way; it is joy." (I repeated "joy" many times.) I told her I was reminded of Isaiah 61 when God said that He would replace mourning with gladness and ashes for a crown of beauty. By now, I could see tears in her eyes. Then I said, "I see broken relationships, but God is going to fill a gap or an empty space with someone and all this would be done with joy." By then she was really in tears, and she said, "Wow, I needed that; thank you so much."

I was amazed to hear Christian music in the restaurant and I told the cashier how much I appreciated it. She said, "Thanks; we don't always get positive remarks." Then I proceeded to tell her that sometimes God speaks and I think He is speaking about you right now. "I see you taking a stand for God many times. It hasn't always been a positive experience, and during earlier years you weren't that positive, but God has taken you along beside Him in order for you to get to know Him. You have been tried and proven. You've been in the fire, brought out, and in the fire again." (By this time, she was in tears.) "You are now a woman of peace and joy. I see that Isaiah 61 is a unique chapter for you. Now you can set others free and bind up the brokenhearted." She was overwhelmed with His Presence and thanked me.

I usually get some kind of a response. Sometimes it is earth shaking and sometimes, like these two cases, Papa is touching people in a deep and special way. I brought the Kingdom. You can do it, too.

You were created for this. You are supernatural. You are a son or daughter of Almighty God, Creator, King. You bring the Kingdom wherever you go. You are life! You have no sin, shame, or guilt! You join Jesus in His work and do what He is doing! *You are a part of this Elijah Generation preparing the way for Jesus' return. His return is valid whether He comes in the clouds or comes with revival.* He is returning! And you are a wise virgin with plenty of oil, the oil of His anointing, because you are a deep well of Christ.

Determine to be intentional in your pursuit of Papa's love. Stop doing church the same old way. Transform your passion into relationship with Him. Find a prophetic group of sons and daughters going after His Presence. Learn how to hear Papa more clearly. Learn and ascertain a level of healing, miracles, and signs and wonders. Go, and do what you see Papa doing. **Let no one destroy your vision to live as a lion!**

You know of the showdown with Elijah and Ahab on Mt. Carmel. There had been a drought for three years. In 1 Kings 18, Elijah presented himself fearlessly to Ahab in Jezebel's territory. Jezebel had annihilated many of the prophets of God. The scene at Mt. Carmel amazes us with Elijah's obedience to

God. Elijah was at the right place at the right time. His obedience is impeccable down to the twelve stones for the sacrifice, the water drenching the sacrifice, filling the trench. Then came the climatic moment: He called fire down from heaven in the name of Yahweh! Why? What was the reason for this big showdown?

"So these people will know that you, O Lord, are God, and that you are turning their hearts back again." (vs. 37)

Why the Elijah Generation? Why the miracles, the glory, the prophecy? God is after your heart and the heart of others. He's after your heart! Mahesh Chavda has said on many occasions, "Only love can make a miracle."

Get on this train! Get into the River! Get into His Presence! Release His Anointing! Be a lion!

At the beginning of this book, I purposely referenced the two BIG questions that everyone asks: *Who am I?* and *What am I doing?* The more divine question is one Jesus asked Peter, "Who do you say that I am?" (Matt. 16:15) Peter's response is a great example of revelation: "for this was not revealed to you by man, but by my Father in heaven" (v.17). Upon Peter's revelation that Jesus is the Christ, the Son of the Living God, the church is built and keys of the Kingdom are given. *Papa's desire is to give you revelation that will change your whole being.* He will give you the keys to the Kingdom, not found in a book or another Bible study, but in Him. Jesus died for this!

HE WAS THE LION THAT BECAME THE LAMB SO THAT LAMBS COULD BECOME LIONS.

I pray...that you receive revelation from the Father, to KNOW Papa through INTIMACY; that you would become a LION with Kingdom privileges and rights.

YOU ARE A SON! YOU ARE A LION.

APPENDIX

RISING DEGREE OF SPIRITUAL GROWTH
Spiritual growth is dependent upon living in His glory

Key: This chart represents an increase in God's glory as one grows and matures in Christ.

```
GOD'S PRESENCE              GOD'S GLORY
THE INTANGIBLE----|-------------THE TANGIBLE------------------|Flesh cannot survive
(Subjective)        |              (Objective)                  |
                    |                                           |
                    |                                           | ETERNITY
                    |
                    |                        Ready to die for Christ.
                    |
                    |                        Holy Spirit led.
                    |
                    |                        Ambassador (signs and wonders).
                    |
                    |                        Encapsulate the love of Papa.
                    |
                    |                        God creates a passion inside of the disciple.
                    |
                    |                        Incorporation into the Body.
                    |
                    |                        Has problems but with help, initiates a lifestyle of obedience.
                    |
                    |                        Begins a process of growth in the Word. Hears God.
                    |
                    | BAPTISM, DELIVERANCE, BAPTISM IN THE HOLY SPIRIT.
```

Repents and confesses Jesus. Feels His Presence.

Positive attitude towards Jesus.

A personal problem.

Touched by God through circumstances or by others numerous times. Hears the Gospel.

Aware of a Supreme Being, but no effective knowledge of Jesus.

Birth.

GOD'S PRESENCE-|-----------GOD'S GLORY--------------------|--------------------------

RISING DEGREE OF REVELATION
Hearing God is dependent upon living in His glory

Key: This chart represents an increase in God's glory as one hears God more clearly.

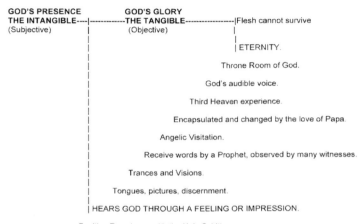

GOD'S PRESENCE   **GOD'S GLORY**
THE INTANGIBLE----|------------THE TANGIBLE-----------------|Flesh cannot survive
(Subjective)   (Objective)

| ETERNITY.

Throne Room of God.

God's audible voice.

Third Heaven experience.

Encapsulated and changed by the love of Papa.

Angelic Visitation.

Receive words by a Prophet, observed by many witnesses.

Trances and Visions.

Tongues, pictures, discernment.

| HEARS GOD THROUGH A FEELING OR IMPRESSION.

Positive Experience with the Holy Spirit!

Hears God when around other prophetic followers.

Believes that God is answering your prayers.

An Epiphany: A Scripture, song, or sign gives you an "aha" moment.

Other believers hear for you and pour into you.

New Birth in Christ.

GOD'S PRESENCE-|----------GOD'S GLORY----------------------|---------------------------

RISING DEGREE OF LOVE, LIFE, AND ANOINTING WITH PAPA
A personal relationship with God is dependent upon living in His glory

Key: This chart represents an increase in God's glory as one grows in relationship with Him and His Kingdom.

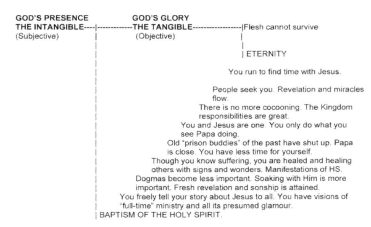

GOD'S PRESENCE   GOD'S GLORY
THE INTANGIBLE----|------------THE TANGIBLE-----------------|Flesh cannot survive
(Subjective) | (Objective) |

                    | | ETERNITY

                    You run to find time with Jesus.

                    People seek you. Revelation and miracles
                      flow.
                    There is no more cocooning. The Kingdom
                      responsibilities are great.
                    You and Jesus are one. You only do what you
                      see Papa doing.
                    Old "prison buddies" of the past have shut up. Papa
                      is close. You have less time for yourself.
                    Though you know suffering, you are healed and healing
                      others with signs and wonders. Manifestations of HS.
                    Dogmas become less important. Soaking with Him is more
                      important. Fresh revelation and sonship is attained.
                    You freely tell your story about Jesus to all. You have visions of
                      "full-time" ministry and all its presumed glamour.
                    BAPTISM OF THE HOLY SPIRIT.

          Tongue-tied charismatic.

          Experience group healings.

          Experience the tangible presence of God and hear God with other anointed hearers.

          Great Body Life—experience passionate worship.

          Discipled: Taught cognitively—Scripture, doctrine, God, and sonship.

New Birth in Christ.

GOD'S PRESENCE-|------------GOD'S GLORY--------------------|----------------------------

RISING DEGREE OF SUFFERING WITH VICTORY
Suffering's sting is severely mitigated living in His glory

Key: This chart represents an increase in God's glory as it relates to suffering.

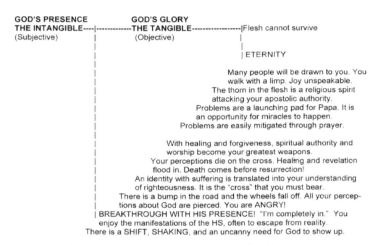

GOD'S PRESENCE   **GOD'S GLORY**
THE INTANGIBLE----|-------------THE TANGIBLE-----------------|Flesh cannot survive
(Subjective)   (Objective)

| ETERNITY

Many people will be drawn to you. You
walk with a limp. Joy unspeakable.
The thorn in the flesh is a religious spirit
attacking your apostolic authority.
Problems are a launching pad for Papa. It is
an opportunity for miracles to happen.
Problems are easily mitigated through prayer.

With healing and forgiveness, spiritual authority and
worship become your greatest weapons.
Your perceptions die on the cross. Healing and revelation
flood in. Death comes before resurrection!
An identity with suffering is translated into your understanding
of righteousness. It is the "cross" that you must bear.
There is a bump in the road and the wheels fall off. All your perceptions about God are pierced. You are ANGRY!
| BREAKTHROUGH WITH HIS PRESENCE! "I'm completely in." You
enjoy the manifestations of the HS, often to escape from reality.
There is a SHIFT, SHAKING, and an uncanny need for God to show up.

Reoccurring problem. It's hard to break some sinful habits.

A breakthrough occurs with help from the saints and Jesus.

A major problem occurs. You are disenchanted with all this religion.

Worried about salvation and challenges of life.

Accept Christ.

GOD'S PRESENCE-|-----------GOD'S GLORY--------------------|---------------------------

RISING DEGREE OF INNER HEALING
Inner healing is dependent upon more of His glory

Key: This chart represents an intensity of God's glory as one is healed.

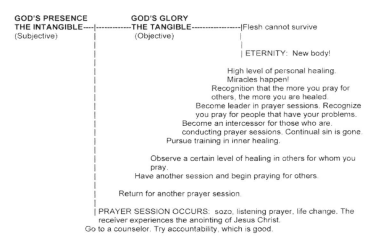

GOD'S PRESENCE
THE INTANGIBLE----|------------THE TANGIBLE-----------------|Flesh cannot survive
(Subjective) | (Objective) |
                   | |
                   | | ETERNITY: New body!
                   |
                   | High level of personal healing.
                   | Miracles happen!
                   | Recognition that the more you pray for
                   | others, the more you are healed.
                   | Become leader in prayer sessions. Recognize
                   | you pray for people that have your problems.
                   | Become an intercessor for those who are.
                   | conducting prayer sessions. Continual sin is gone.
                   | Pursue training in inner healing.
                   |
                   | Observe a certain level of healing in others for whom you
                   | pray.
                   | Have another session and begin praying for others.
                   |
                   | Return for another prayer session.
                   |
                   | PRAYER SESSION OCCURS: sozo, listening prayer, life change. The
                   | receiver experiences the anointing of Jesus Christ.
                   Go to a counselor. Try accountability, which is good.

        Receive healing by other followers for your problems.

    Receive a cognitive approach to healing.

    Read a book on healing. Ask Jesus to heal and He does, some.

   "I'm just fine." We don't need inner healing. We're covered by the blood of Jesus.

Born again!

GOD'S PRESENCE-|-----------GOD'S GLORY---------------------|----------------------------

RISING DEGREE OF IDENTITY
Revelation of sonship comes with the rising intensity of His glory

Key: This chart represents an increase in spiritual intensity as one grows in sonship.

GOD'S PRESENCE   **GOD'S GLORY**
THE INTANGIBLE----|------------THE TANGIBLE-----------------|Flesh cannot survive
(Subjective) | (Objective) |

                    | | ETERNITY: Rev. 22.

         | Frequently worshiping with the 24
         | elders.
         | Walking shoulder-to-shoulder. Christ in you
         | is the hope of glory (Col.1:27). Friendship.
         | Becoming the Apple of His Eye. Forsaking all
         | others. Intimacy is more important than anything
         | We are sons of light receiving revelation (Jn.12:36;
         | Jn 16:14,15; Jn.10:9.10).
         | **Revelation:** Moving from servanthood to sonship
         | (Gal. 4:5).
         | **Integration:** To know Him is to experience Him. Becoming
         | sons and daughters (Rms. 8:14-17; Gal. 4: 4-7).
         | **Christ Actualization:** Healing from wounds. Renouncing lies
         | and half-truths.
         | Putting off the old self and clothing yourself with Christ (Eph. 4:22,
         | 23; Col. 2: 9-15).
         | DILEMMA: THE FEAR OF GOD BEGINS TO OUTWEIGH FLESHLY
         DESIRES. SHAKING!
      Fear of Man is prevalent. Cultural relevance and peer pressure is tantamount

You know about God but fail to know His voice (Jn. 10:4).

Self actualization: Realizing who you are and your potential.

-Born again: I am Yours and You are mine.

Humanistic Identity: "self-image". I am good! (But why do I feel so bad?)

False Identity: I am a victim, inadequate, bad, ugly.

GOD'S PRESENCE-|------------GOD'S GLORY---------------------|---------------------------

ABOUT THE AUTHOR

DWIGHT HAYMON and his wife, Candy, have served in ministry for 37 years. Dwight earned his BA, Atlanta Christian College; M.Div., Lincoln Christian Seminary; with additional studies at Columbia Theological Seminary and a concentrated period at Fuller Theological Seminary.

Dwight and Candy, pastors and founders of Lifegate International (Atlanta, GA), have pastored established churches, planted churches, and served churches through leadership under pastors. Their passion is to release the Father's Heart, listening to His voice with a prophetic ministry of hope and healing to all people.

The Haymons have three children and two grandchildren and reside in Atlanta, Georgia.

Lifegate International: www.lifegateinternational.com
Lifegate International: www.lifegateinafrica.org

Made in the USA
San Bernardino, CA
29 January 2014